JEWISH MANUAL

OR

PRACTICAL INFORMATION IN
JEWISH & MODERN COOKERY
WITH A COLLECTION OF
VALUABLE RECIPES & HINTS
RELATING TO THE TOILETTE

EDITED BY A LADY

A FACSIMILE OF THE FIRST
JEWISH COOKBOOK IN ENGLISH
PUBLISHED IN 1846

INTRODUCTION BY CHAIM RAPHAEL

NIGHTINGALE BOOKS

Introduction copyright © 1983 by Chaim Raphael
Cover design copyright © 1983 by Adrianne Onderdonk Dudden
Printed in the United States of America
All rights reserved.

Library of Congress Cataloging in Publication Data
Lady.
The Jewish manual, or, Practical information in
Jewish & modern cookery with a collection of valuable
recipes & hints relating to the toilette.
A facsimile of the first Jewish cookbook in English
published in 1846, with a new introduction by Chaim Raphael.
Reprint. Originally published: London: T. & W. Boone, 1846.
1. Cookery, Jewish.   2. Beauty, Personal.   3. London
(England)—Social life and customs. I. Raphael, Chaim.
II. Title. III. Title: Jewish manual.
TX724.L3   *1983*   641.5′676   *83-2405*
ISBN 0-911389-00-8

COVER ILLUSTRATION:
from a micrograph formed of biblical verses for
Blessings for a Wedding and Pidyon ha-Ben,
prepared for Rabbi Naftali M. Adler, London, 1849.
Courtesy of Rare Book Collection,
Jewish Theological Seminary of America.

NIGHTINGALE BOOKS
New York   ·   Cold Spring, N.Y.

PUBLISHER'S NOTE

We discovered *The Jewish Manual* while looking for something else in the Jewish Division of the New York Public Library. The slender volume seemed to us not only enchanting but also a bit of history. Through some fascinating research in contemporary documents, we were delighted to be able to confirm its authenticity as the first Jewish cookbook published in English. As such it reflects the social and economic status of Jews in England in the mid-nineteenth century.

Much has been written recently about East European Jews, Russian Jews, German Jews, but the general public knows little about the English Jews. It was with this in mind that we asked Chaim Raphael to write an introduction placing this community in the context of English history, customs, and social acceptance.

Social acceptance notwithstanding—and Jews were socially integrated in English society—this cookbook constantly emphasizes that it was written for the Jewish kitchen. The sophisticated culinary knowledge of the editor is seen in her familiarity with dishes of the outstanding chefs of the day as well as her use of technical terms. The term "to lard," for example, is used in its most general sense, meaning to add fat (p. 51). Recipes for velouté and bechamel sauces are given because "they are so frequently mentioned in modern cookery . . . although they are not appropriate for the Jewish kitchen" (p. 31).

The Editor's Preface and Observations for the Cook might, for all their elegant phrases, have been written today, suggesting, as they do, the importance of creativity, moderation, and "graceful originality." It is, says our lady editor, "the unfailing attribute of a superior mind to turn its attention occasionally to the lesser objects of life, aware how greatly they contribute to its harmony and its happiness."

Small as this volume is, it has presented a challenge in our research—first to check its authenticity and then to locate historical and pictorial material. For their help in this journey back in time, we would like to thank the following individuals and organizations: Leonard Gold, director of the Jewish Division, and Helga Borck, assistant for Resources, Collection Management and Development Division, of The New York Public Library; Nadia Kahan, reference librarian, Special Collections, Jewish Theological Seminary of America; Rachelle Gribetz of The Mendel Gottesman Library of Hebraica-Judaica, Yeshiva University; Esther Eidensohn of the Blaustein Library, American Jewish Committee; the staff of The Library of the YIVO Institute for Jewish Research in New York; the staffs of the Thomas J. Watson Library and the Department of Prints and Photographs Study Room of The Metropolitan Museum of Art; Machsike Hadas of Bibliotheca Judaica Simonsoniana of the Royal Library of Copenhagen; Rabbi Reuven Siegel; Dorothea Straus; Adrianne Onderdonk Dudden; Tom White of Haddon Craftsmen; Sheila Tennenbaum.

And a special thanks to the staff of the Department of Public Information of The Metropolitan Museum of Art for their many kindnesses . . . and to person or persons unknown who thought to donate the original copy of *The Jewish Manual* not to the rubbish heap but to the Jewish Division of The New York Public Library.

Ruth L. Gales and Lila T. Gold

NOTE: We discovered that in 1846 the printer made an error in numbering the pages of *The Jewish Manual*. While page number 224 is followed by page number 235, there is no interruption in the text.

Mr. Raphael's latest book on a Jewish theme is *The Springs of Jewish Life* (Basic Books, 1982). Earlier books include *Memoirs of a Special Case, A Feast of History,* and *Encounters with the Jewish People.* As a mystery writer, under the name Jocelyn Davey, his latest book is *Murder in Paradise* (Walker & Co.).

THE HISTORY AND
THE MYSTERY OF
THE JEWISH MANUAL

As a diversion from writing histories, I also write mysteries; and I cannot imagine these two interests brought together more happily than in the utterly charming cookbook of 1846, *The Jewish Manual,* that Ruth Gales and Lila Gold have now brought back to life in this facsimile edition.

To find an elegant and sophisticated Jewish cookbook published fifteen years before Mrs. Beeton's classic work, *The Book of Household Management,* is surprise enough; and it is particularly satisfying that the recipes in the book are all couched in very practical terms. As in any good Victorian household, domestic help is envisaged and menus are expected to be ample; but everything is scaled to "normal" living, unlike the legendary extravagances that were to appear in Mrs. Beeton's book.

Even without the history and mystery embedded in *The Jewish Manual,* it is a delight merely to turn the pages to see what a Jewish housewife in early Victorian London put on her table, what instructions she gave her cook, and perhaps above all how she talked about it. At times one feels *plus ça change, plus c'est la même chose;* but much more often the scene is full of surprises. This is perhaps not so frequent with the staple dishes; but even they are half-frenchified in presentation. As this is a manual of *Jewish* cookery and includes nothing to offend *kosher* principles, it is not surprising to find some inescapably Jewish dishes, notably for Passover. But it is quite obvious that many of the dishes which have come to personify Jewish traditional eating—like bagels and lox—are notably absent. Nonetheless, some apparent absentees—like gefilte fish and chopped liver—can be tracked down in flimsy disguise, while on every page of this book, now nearly 140 years old, are dishes which seem to be rooted in a very un-Jewish background.

But behind this, one is aware of a flood of questions. The underlying *history* question is: who was this book written for? Most of the Jews of England today, like the Jews of America, think of their nineteenth-century ancestors in Russian-Jewish terms, as described so graphically in Irving Howe's *World of Our Fathers*. There were a few high-born Sephardi families here and there; but books are prepared for a solid clientele, and the social setting of mass Jewry was, for a long time, utterly remote in ambience from the sophisticated elegancies of *The Jewish Manual*. Yet for some reason, there was an audience for this book in the England of 1846; and the historian in me wants to explain why this throws a powerful light on the dynamics of Jewish history.

Unfolding this is like opening a Chinese box, for within the history one is aware of a mystery. Who was "A Lady" to whom the book is credited?

*

The special character of *The Jewish Manual* cannot be understood without recognizing that English Jewry in the 1840s had stabilized, for a few decades, into something unique in Jewish history. Every country in the world in which Jews have settled in some number has produced, at some point, a form of Jewish life which is unique in the way it has adopted but also transmogrified the background. This was true of medieval Jews in the Golden Age of Spain, which ended so sadly in the Expulsion of 1492. Special forms of Jewish life were developed equally by the Jews of Renaissance Italy, nineteenth-century Russia, and early twentieth-century Germany. Coming closer to our own day, could any community be more distinctive socially, politically, economically, and intellectually than that of the Jews of the United States? In these judgments, the historian has to assess how far the uniqueness of what emerges is due to innate Jewish qualities and how far to something very distinctive in the host culture.

England in the 1840s had emerged as the world's greatest financial and economic power, a development in which a number of well-established Jewish families had played a small but significant part. Britain's unparalleled leadership, especially in industrial production and trade, was due to begin a decline in the next few decades, yielding the first place increasingly in many fields to Continental Europe and ultimately, of course, to the United States. This change, which began in the 1880s, made itself felt decisively by World War I and was intensified through World War II; but it is still fair to say that for a full century after the 1840s the Victorian preeminence continued to trail clouds of some kind of glory and influence, particularly in the realm of the arts and gracious living. And here, of course, is a hint at why this gracious 1846 manual covering food and a lady's toilette and some basics of taste and style exercises its charm simply as a reflection of those far-off days when England generated an air of quality and effortless superiority.

If a Jewish cookbook of this period captures the early Victorian charm, it is also a sign of the very unusual character of the *Jewish* community of England as it existed at this time, when earlier immigration had given way to stability. We are so aware today that Jewish history during the last century was characterized by a flow (and sometimes a flood) of impoverished immigrants into western countries that it comes as a surprise to find that there had been virtually no Jewish inflow into England in the first half of the nineteenth century. Within forty years of the *Manual*'s date, the Jews of England—like the Jews of the United States—began to expand in numbers and change in character through the immigration that followed the Russian pogroms of 1881. But by the 1840s the Jews of England had become a settled community, small in number and with an elitist tone that somehow managed to combine for the elite and the rising bourgeoisie both a widespread social freedom and a powerful sense of Jewish identity and loyalty.

In these terms alone one can begin to understand the genesis of a manual that, as the Preface explains, would offer a cooking guide "to all the receipts peculiar to the Jewish people" while at the same time cover, for the huge meals of Victorian times, both all "the plain English dishes" and also "such French ones as are now in general use at all refined modern tables." One has to recognize, within the purpose, both a strong practical aim and a sense of *noblesse oblige.* England's Jewish community at this time numbered only some 30,000, of whom two-thirds lived in the heart of London while the rest were scattered in very small provincial groups, originally at seaports, but increasingly in the growing industrial towns. Within the London community, leadership lay in the hands of a "cousinhood" of families who had risen steadily in wealth and influence. Some of their ancestors had been in England since the second half of the seventeenth century, with a powerful infusion in the second half of the eighteenth century. The most successful of the founding fathers, rising to wealth in the "square mile" of the City, had enjoyed a form of social ease with the "upper classes"—the aristocracy and the royal family—which was extremely rare for Jews elsewhere. Yet they had ardent Jewish loyalties, expressed both in religious faith and in social responsibility toward their less-favored coreligionists. And as history shows everywhere, they were noted for social work and charity on a munificent scale, helping the poor and needy in the country at large.

The English quality of this elite comes out very clearly if one contrasts the mid-nineteenth century life there with that of the United States. There were, of course, some personal and financial links between the Jews of both countries; but the character of life and the opportunities for the future could not have been more different. In the United States, the Jews were taking part in a huge open-ended adventure, with little central cohesion. From the beginning, the United States had been an immigrant country, with the social separation and the sense of experiment that sustained this process. In England, by contrast, the Jews now domiciled there felt that their aim was to be absorbed quietly into a settled pattern, with no sense of upheaval and adventure. Absorption did not mean losing their Jewish identity; indeed, the social pattern of English life allowed for, and even encouraged, the eccentric alien, as was seen supremely in the career of Disraeli. Much of this was to change when relatively large-scale immigration began at the end of the century. But even then, the liberalism—and stuffiness—of Victorian standards continued to be the norm for many decades; and it is significant that the "old" families who had been in the forefront in mid-Victorian times continued—and still continue—to play a leading role in Jewish institutions. In this sense, the *Manual* of 1846 might still carry some recognizable tone for them, even if they are not as attentive as their ancestors were to the strict rules of traditional Jewish eating.

Taking a metaphor from food, it could be said that these "leading" Jewish families and the bourgeoisie rising steadily behind them were in the unusual but pleasant situation of having their cake and eating it. They were able to settle (with some hiccups) into an ancient established society, with long and rich cultural traditions potent for their enjoyment. At the same time they were taking root in England at a time when this stable society, built on a basis of ancient churches and villages, a radiant countryside, military and naval independence, and a solid respect for the rule of law, was now poised for imperial and economic expansion, as revolutionary in its own way as the opening-up, later, of the United States. That the early English Jews arrived when they did and were able to strengthen their base in this way, especially in the City, was not a coincidence. The expansion of Empire, and the Industrial Revolution gathering pace toward the end of the eighteenth century, were to offer a special role to some of the new arrivals; and as we outline the story, albeit briefly, a clue may be dropped here and there to the solution of the mystery: who was "A Lady," responsible for *The Jewish Manual?*

*

The Jews who began to settle in England in the second half of the seventeenth century were just one echo of the great upheavals that had affected the Jews of Europe when their rich and long-established life in Spain and Portugal had been brought to an end through persecution and expulsion. The passionate Catholicism of Spain had led many Jews into conversion, though often only superficially. After the official expulsion of all Jews from Spain and Portugal at the end of the fifteenth century and the increasing menace of the Inquisition to secret Jews (who became known as

"Marranos"), thousands of Jews who were now in flight carried their high culture (and their Spanish and Portuguese nostalgia) with them to many parts of the world. Some settled in North Africa, Italy, Greece, Turkey, and the Holy Land. Others found their way north to Holland, recently freed from Spanish rule. The link with England was to start here.

When the great sweeps of history have involved Jews, the process has usually been multidimensional. The Christian conquest of Spain led to the expulsion of all Jews in 1492. But 1492 was also the year in which Columbus discovered America; and Jewish history was soon on the move in new directions. Portugal, where Marrano Jews continued to play a major role in science, politics, and finance, was opening up the world through exploration. Holland, where many of these "Sephardi" (Spanish and Portuguese) Jews put down roots, became central to the furthering of trade and development all over the world.

The participation of Jews in these historical developments was not, of course, limited to Sephardim. The increasingly fruitful settlement of Sephardi Jews in Holland brought in "Ashkenazi" (German) Jews, who drew on a long and rich experience of their own. If the Sephardi elite put a special mark on Amsterdam at the beginning, the mixture of both traditions was potent there for the future, as it was in Hamburg and many of the towns of northwest Europe. But the Sephardim have a particularly romantic role in this story, especially in relation to the origins of the present Jewish community of England.

A small number of Jews had originally settled in England in Norman times, but after being exploited by successive kings in lending and tax-gathering roles, they had been expelled by royal decree in 1290. We hear of a few Jews who lived in England in Elizabethan times, though usually in the guise of Portuguese Catholics. In the era of Oliver Cromwell, who was Lord Protector of England in 1653–58, some Sephardi families were living in London more openly; and in 1656 a leading Dutch rabbi, Menasseh ben Israel, petitioned Cromwell to revoke the Expulsion Order of 1290 and give Jews permission to reside in England officially and practice their religion. In the event, the Order was not officially revoked; but those Jews already in England were allowed religious rights: to meet for prayers and have a burial ground. It was on this relaxed informal basis that the Jewish community began to develop in its quiet way, though without full political rights until 1858, two hundred years later.

*

Political rights were less important to begin with than the freedom to live openly as Jews in a country that was poised for great prosperity. The pattern of English-Jewish life which ultimately produced the *Manual* as a by-product in 1846, took shape during the eighteenth century while Britain was expanding into a great empire, taking in her stride the loss of the American colonies in 1776. English Jews of the time, though not numerous, were already providing an important element in finance and trade, with Sephardi families often in the lead because of their wide international relationships. But the Ashkenazim who were following them into England would, even in the early years, equal if not surpass their financial importance. It was not long, in fact, before the two "clans" began to intermarry, with this "cousinhood" reaching full force in the nineteenth century.

Inevitably it is the Sephardi names—Mocatta, Henriques, Lindo, and so on—which have remained distinctive. A number of the early Sephardi settlers had arrived via Holland but were reinforced as time went on by a constant flow of ex-Marranos from Spain and Portugal, as well as by fellow-Sephardim who made their way to England via the West Indies (e.g., the Lousadas), Italy (the Montefiores), and other places. Except for Rothschild, the Ashkenazim did not bear names that emerged with the same resonance, but they were soon noteworthy in the City and soci-

ety. The outstanding merchant bankers and gov-
ernment brokers toward the end of the eighteenth
century were two Ashkenazi brothers called
Goldsmid. With an even plainer name, the man
around whom the whole world of upper-class
Jewry was to revolve was an Ashkenazi-Dutch
Jew called Levy Barent Cohen, who arrived in
London in 1770 with close links to the Goldsmids
and other leading finance families. It illustrates the
cousinhood to note that one of Mr. Cohen's
daughters married Nathan Mayer Rothschild,
founder of the English branch of the family, while
another married young Moses Montefiore. Two
more of Mr. Cohen's numerous brood married
two children of Moses Samuel, also active in the
City as a banker and broker. Family links continued to be forged this way. "Blood and money
flowed in a small circle which opened up for a
time to admit a Beddington, a Montagu, a Frank-
lin, a Sassoon, or anyone else who attained rank
and fortune, and then snapped shut again."[1]

With *The Jewish Manual* in mind, one notes
that sumptuous banquets were a feature of the
time, and in Jewish high society there was a mixture of Jews and Gentiles. Lord Nelson, accom-
panied by Lady Hamilton, was a frequent guest,
with other members of the aristocracy, at the huge
country house of Asher Goldsmid at Morden (near
London). We are told by a diarist that on one such

1. Chaim Bermant, *The Cousinhood* (New York: Macmillan,
1973), p. 1.

occasion young Moses Montefiore, who was very devout, recited the full version of the Grace After Meals in Hebrew; Nelson may well have wondered if it would ever end.[2]

Not all the cousinhood were equally pious; and we soon hear in the eighteenth century of the ultimate sacrilege: baptism, with or without some intermarriage with Christians. The historian Cecil Roth was fond of demonstrating, with a certain amount of impish glee, that this process has deeply affected a large part of the British aristocracy; and Chaim Bermant offers some examples in his entertaining book *The Cousinhood.* The daughter of the heiress Kitty da Costa married the second Viscount Galway, whose descendants included the Marquess of Crewe. Descendants of the Sephardi family Franco included Lord Ludlow and Viscount Bledisloe. The Duke of St. Albans is a descendant of Jacob Israel Bernal (as well as Charles II by one of his mistresses). Yet though the lists of conversion, infiltration, and intermarriage are quite long, they give a misleading picture by themselves. The great majority of the leading Jews of this time remained loyal to their ancient faith.

This all emerges in Victorian times in reports and advertisements appearing in the *Jewish Chronicle,* a weekly newspaper founded in 1841 and still important today in its role as reflecting the character of English-Jewish society. Sometimes the re-

2. Bermant, p. 22.

ports from the period of the *Manual* have a political angle, as in a story, in October 1844, of a dinner at the London Tavern "of nearly 300 gentlemen" to support the candidature of David Salomons to be an alderman of the City of London. (He was, in fact, elected and became the first Jewish Lord Mayor of London in 1855.) The menu of that dinner is not given; but when Mr. J. Myers, "Cook and Confectioner of Aldgate" (a Jewish area), advertises in the *Chronicle,* the Bill of Fare he announces is a three-course meal of mock turtle soup, salmon and codfish, fowls and tongues, pigeon pies, turkey, capons, and goslings—all for twelve shillings and six pence, including a great array of desserts.

The Jewish middle classes were clearly on the rise. The *Chronicle* advertisements illustrate that many "ordinary" Jews were now beginning to enjoy the good things of life. Not all the events publicized there were necessarily restricted to the Jewish community. One wonders, for example, about the "Grand Ball and Concert" advertised in the issue of November 10, 1848, at which Mr. Chopin had consented to play some of his compositions on the pianoforte. No such doubts exist over the song recital by the Swedish nightingale Jenny Lind, reported in the issue of September 17, 1847. A long and lyrical account explains that it was a benefit "in behalf of the Funds of the Bir-

mingham Hebrew National School." Ticket sales
raised the record sum of £1800, "exclusive of the
very liberal donation of the Rothschild family,
who patronized the concert." Five years later, as
it happened, Jenny Lind married a Jewish business-
man from Hamburg called Otto Goldschmidt,
which fits in nicely.

Not that these elegant and artistic functions
were typical of the condition of Jews as a whole.
London at the beginning of the nineteenth century
included among its masses many poor Jews who
eked out the charity they received from their
richer coreligionists by scratching a living as "old
clothesmen," street peddlers, and practitioners of
many shady pursuits. Many humble but respect-
able Jews above them in the social scale—shop-
keepers, tailors, watchmakers, and other skilled or
semiskilled workmen—showed the trend that
would grow as the century moved on.

The brilliant research of the social historian
Vivian D. Lipman has shown how far this rising
movement had progressed by mid-century, when
the *Manual* was published. Through an analysis of
households (partly from census information on
how many servants were kept) and relief rolls, it
appears that the 20,000 Jews of London consisted
roughly of 1,000 who were "upper or upper-
middle class," 6,000 who formed the rest of the
middle class, some 7,500 who were "lower class"

but not on relief, and 5,500 on occasional or regular relief. Furthermore, Lipman notes this startling change: at the beginning of the century, the poor were the great majority and the middle class hardly existed; by 1880, the middle class (judged by earnings and at least one servant) comprised nearly half the community, and there had been a continual decline in hawking, peddling, and other typical poor Jewish occupations. "This was partly due to the efforts of those concerned to rise from peddling to shopkeeping; partly to the efforts of the community to apprentice boys to traders; and partly to undercutting by the poor Irish immigrants of the 1840s and 1850s."[3]

*

The setting and the central purpose of publishing *The Jewish Manual* in 1846 is now, I hope, becoming clear. It was basically a gesture *de haut en bas*, but without the slightest touch of snobbery. To understand this, one should see the *Manual* in two facets. At one level, it was addressed to households who already kept a fine Victorian table and who needed to be shown how their servants could achieve the highest standards while still adhering to strict Jewish observance. At another level, it offered a mirror of high taste to those just rising in the social scale and in need of a helping hand. This explains the section at the end of the *Manual* called "The Toilette," which gives extremely

3. "The Anglo-Jewish Community in Victorian Society," in *Studies in the Cultural Life of the Jews of England,* Folklore Research Center Studies, vol. 5 (Hebrew University of Jerusalem, 1975), p. 155.

practical advice on complexion, hair, dress, and such, but warns the reader throughout against the flamboyance that is often characteristic of women beginning to move in higher social circles. This forty-three page section by "A Lady" is so thorough and deeply felt that it almost seems to be a major motive in composing the book.

But who was "A Lady"? Not many of the leading Jewish families bore formal titles at that stage, but we may still keep this in mind as a possible clue. Noting other clues which seem to make their mark in the text, we might be sure that it was someone who had herself lived a life of high privilege, yet was simple and unspoiled. She was clearly a sincere Jewess, not merely observant of *kosher* principles but devoted to the welfare of fellow-Jews throughout the country and indeed everywhere.

Looking for the moment merely at internal evidence—with external evidence to come later—is there a clue in the dishes described as to whether she was a Sephardi or Ashkenazi? The Preface talks of a strong tradition: "all the best receipts, hitherto bequeathed only by memory or manuscript"; and among these "receipts" are both German and Spanish elements. Among the sweets, names are often Sephardi, as in the elaborate confection "bola d'amor," and the sweet yeast cake "bola d'Hispaniola." On the German side, we hear of sauer kraut and kugel; and it may be German that there is a recipe for rump steak (acceptable to observant Jews if properly porged). The cookbook also recommends venison, partridge, and pheasant, presumably hunted or trapped pacifically, and with one's own *shohet* (ritual slaughterer) on hand to dispatch the animal or bird in accord with required Jewish methods. (Perhaps this is a clue to encourage us to look for a family that always traveled with its own *shohet*.) Beyond the Sephardi-Ashkenazi alternatives there are Dutch dishes which could be either, as in a fish dish ("an excellent receipt for stewed fish in the Dutch fashion"), or "waflers" (waffles), for which one used "wafler irons" obtainable "at any good ironmonger of the Hebrew persuasion." And very much felt is the new English influence, as in mock turtle soup or "muligatawnay."

We know that we cannot expect East European dishes like borscht at this stage: the Russian-Jewish immigrants do not arrive until the 1880s. But it is intriguing to see that some dishes associated with the Russian "world of our fathers" do emerge. If there is no gefilte fish, there are fish balls. There is a "Luction" cake, which is perhaps a "lokshen" pudding. There is a dessert cheesecake, though made without cheese: the name originally meant a cake *shaped* like a cheese. There is no dish called "cholent" (Yiddish for a stew kept hot over Sabbath), but a dish called "Commean" is the same thing, the word being a corruption of the Hebrew word *chamin* (hot).

But if the authoress throws her net wide, she does seem to favor Sephardi and Ashkenazi sources, and indeed one dish is actually called "German or Spanish puffs." On this basis alone, one might conjecture that she belonged to a mixed Sephardi-Ashkenazi household, a common feature of the cousinhood. In many fields, indeed, the old distinctions had been overcome. The new weekly newspaper, the *Jewish Chronicle,* reported joint endeavors for the sake of the community as a whole. In the first Reform synagogue, set up in 1840, the founding fathers, who numbered eighteen, included twelve Sephardim (nine Mocattas, three Montefiores, and three Henriques) and six Ashkenazim, of whom three were Goldsmids. It will obviously be significant for our story of a kosher cookbook that the three reform Montefiores did not include the most eminent member of the clan, Sir Moses Montefiore, who fought Reform Judaism in every way he could.

As Sir Moses's wife, Judith, was Ashkenazi by birth (daughter of Levy Barent Cohen), married to a Sephardi, this would immediately make her the *possible* author. Of course, if one was simply *guessing,* there are quite a few prominent families who could have yielded a lady from a similarly aristocratic background. The "Luction" pudding mentioned earlier is actually called "A Luction, or a Rachael"; and one might wonder if this was an author's hint at Rachel Goldsmid, who was ardently Jewish and had married Count Solomon D'Avigdor, scion of a famous Jewish family from the south of France, when he settled in England in the 1830s. The names became amalgamated and have yielded a line of D'Avigdor-Goldsmids, prominent in public life and headed by a baronet to this day.

Guesswork of this kind is fun for a mystery writer but has its limits. The answer, when it came, had to be based on hard evidence. It was found buried in an issue of the *Jewish Chronicle* of October 10, 1862, discovered more than a hundred years later by the editor of the day, John M. Shaftesley.

*

The story does begin, as was hinted above, with Moses Montefiore, towering figure for the Jews of England and the world in the nineteenth century. Born in 1784, his business interests were not exactly hampered by links with his Mocatta uncles, his brother-in-law Rothschild, and other members of the cousinhood. In this field alone, however, he might have been just one of a number of rich men. His preeminence was linked to two other factors. The first was his decision at the age of forty to

retire from business (though he kept some direc-
torships) in order to devote himself to good
works. The second was that he continued to be
preoccupied with these good works until he died
in 1885 at the age of 101.

In England, he and his wife, Judith, were untir-
ing in their efforts to help the poor and needy; but
his fame soon became worldwide. He was
knighted in 1837; and as a friend of the young
Queen Victoria he enlisted her support when he
went to Damascus in 1840 to secure the release
from prison of a hundred Jews, including fifty-
three children, threatened with execution. They
had been imprisoned and tortured to get them to
confess that they had killed a monk to use his
blood to prepare *matzoh* for Passover—the ancient
"blood libel" that plagued Jews in the Middle
Ages and has never wholly disappeared from the
minds of fanatical Jew-haters. Sir Moses, accom-
panied by his wife, set out for Damascus in almost
royal style to fight the threat there. His mission
attracted awed respect everywhere; and from then
on the Montefiores went everywhere to deal with
trouble in the Jewish world, carrying with them
the prestige of Victorian England on Jewry's behalf. They had paid their first visit to the Holy
Land in 1827, and Sir Moses had thrown himself
into practical work to build up a Jewish community outside the Old City and help train the young

in useful trades. In 1846 they went to Russia and Poland, arousing wild enthusiasm among the Jewish masses. After Judith's death in 1862, Moses went on alone: to Morocco in 1863, to Rumania in 1867. Throughout the world, Montefiore became a magic name.

Was it because she had no children that Judith was so active in helping young people? There is an echo of this in the *Jewish Chronicle* report of 1862, long forgotten but now establishing without any doubt that Lady Montefiore was responsible for *The Jewish Manual*.

The range of Judith's activities is described in a very interesting essay by Sonia Lipman, wife of the social historian Vivian D. Lipman.[4] We see there, incidentally, how much she deplored extravagance, a constant theme in the *Manual*. And with her connection now established, other clues emerge. One is the name given in the *Manual* to "a sweet with gooseberries and cream rice" which is called "a Juditha." On the practicalities of being able to eat partridge and pheasant without offending the laws of *kashrut*, we see that the Montefiores *did* always travel with their own *shohet*. Another very powerful link is seen in the stories of their visits to the Holy Land. In the advice she gives in the *Manual* on how to retain a good complexion, she says: "These are the simple and rational means pursued by the females of the east to obtain a

4. Sonia Lipman, "Judith Montefiore—First Lady of Anglo-Jewry" in *Transactions of the Jewish Historical Society of England,* vol. 21 (1968), pp. 287–303.

smooth and perfect skin." She is even more explic-
it in her recipe for a cosmetic bath, which is from
"the confidential attendant of an English lady who
is in the habit of using it every week."

Judith died in 1862 on Rosh Hashanah. A memorial to her was discussed immediately; and it is
in reporting this that the *Jewish Chronicle* gives us
the secret. In its issue of October 10, 1862, it says
that in his sermon on Yom Kippur the Chief
Rabbi of the Ashkenazi synagogues of England,
the famed Dr. Nathan Marcus Adler, had given
details of the memorial that was to be set up. The
fund would be used to establish dowries to help
suitably trained young Jewish girls to get married;
for Lady Montefiore, he said, "had attached great
importance to the due qualifications of females for
the discharge of domestic duties, in which she
herself excelled, and wrote a book for Jewish
cookery, or at least assisted in its composition."[5]

The mystery is thus solved, but needs a final
word from the Chief Rabbi's sermon to give the
endowment its true Victorian flavor. To raise the
money, says the report, "it is proposed to collect
a fund to which both German and Portuguese
[Ashkenazim and Sephardim] are to contribute,
which even in part might be raised by penny
subscriptions, the interest of which every year
might be used as the marriage portion for a girl
who has distinguished herself by her sustained

5. In announcing his discovery, Mr. Shaftesley discussed
wider aspects of the *Manual* and of Jewish food in England;
see "Culinary Aspects of Anglo-Jewry" in *Studies in the Cultural Life of the Jews in England,* Folklore Research Center
Studies vol. 5 (Hebrew University of Jerusalem, 1975), pp.
367–99.

moral character. The preference is to be given to one who has been employed as a Jewish cook."

How many of these nice young girls used *The Jewish Manual* in their kitchen, we shall never know. It cost five shillings, which was quite expensive; but perhaps each was given a free copy with her dowry. If so, we can be sure that it was likely, in the words of the Preface, "to prove a useful assistant and meet with their lenient, kind and favourable consideration."

THE JEWISH MANUAL;

OR

PRACTICAL INFORMATION IN JEWISH
AND MODERN COOKERY,

WITH A COLLECTION OF

VALUABLE RECIPES & HINTS RELATING TO THE TOILETTE.

EDITED BY A LADY.

LONDON:

T. & W. BOONE, 29, NEW BOND STREET.

1846.

London :
Printed by MELDOLA, CAHN, & CO.,
18, St. Mary Axe, City.

EDITOR'S PREFACE.

———

Among the numerous works on Culinary Science already in circulation, there have been none which afford the slightest insight to the Cookery of the Hebrew kitchen.

Replete as many of these are with information on various important points, they are completely valueless to the Jewish housekeeper, not only on account of prohibited articles and combinations being assumed to be necessary ingredients of nearly every dish, but from the entire absence of all the receipts peculiar to the Jewish people.

This deficiency, which has been so frequently the cause of inconvenience and complaint, we have endeavoured in the present little volume to supply. And in taking upon ourselves the responsibility of introducing it to the notice of our readers, we have been actuated by the hope that it will prove of some practical utility to those for whose benefit it is more particularly designed.

It has been our earnest desire to simplify as much as possible the directions given regarding the rudiments of the art, and to render the receipts which follow, clear, easy, and concise. Our collection will be found to contain all the best receipts, hitherto bequeathed only by memory or manuscript, from one generation to another of the Jewish nation, as well as those which come under the denomination of plain English dishes; and also such French ones as are now in general use at all refined modern tables.

A careful attention has been paid to accuracy and economy in the proportions named, and the receipts may be perfectly depended upon, as we have had the chief part of them tested in our own kitchen and under our own *surveillance.*

All difficult and expensive modes of cookery have been purposely omitted, as more properly belonging to the province of the confectioner, and foreign to the intention of this little work ; the object of which is, to guide the young Jewish housekeeper in the luxury and economy of " The Table," on which so much of the pleasure of social intercourse depends.

The various acquirements, which in the present day are deemed essential to female education, rarely leave much time or inclination for the humble study of household affairs; and it not unfrequently happens, that the mistress of a family understands little more concerning the dinner table over which she presides, than the graceful arrangement of the flowers which adorn it; thus she is incompetent to direct her servant, upon whose inferior judgment and taste she is obliged to depend. She is continually subjected to impositions from her ignorance of what is required for the dishes she selects, while a lavish extravagance, or parsimonious monotony betrays her utter inexperience in all the minute yet indispensible details of elegant hospitality.

However, there are happily so many highly accomplished and intellectual women, whose example proves the compatability of uniting the cultivation of talents with domestic pursuits, that it would be superfluous and presumptuous were we here to urge the propriety and importance of acquiring habits of usefulness and household knowledge, further than to observe that it is the unfailing attribute of a superior mind to turn its attention occasionally to the lesser objects of life, aware how greatly they contribute to its harmony and its happiness.

The *Cuisine* of a woman of refinement, like

her dress or her furniture, is distinguished, not
for its costliness and profusion, but for a pervad-
ing air of graceful originality. She is quite
sensible of the regard due to the reigning
fashion of the day, but her own tasteful discri-
mination is always perceptible. She instinctively
avoids every thing that is hackneyed, vulgar,
and common place, and uniformly succeeds in
pleasing by the judicious novelties she intro-
duces.

We hope, therefore, that this unpretending
little work may not prove wholly unacceptable,
even to those ladies who are not of the Hebrew
persuasion, as it will serve as a sequel to the
books on cookery previously in their possession,
and be the medium of presenting them with
numerous receipts for rare and exquisite compositions, which if uncommemorated by the
genius of Vatêl, Ude, or Carême, are delicious
enough not only to gratify the lovers of good

cheer generally, but to merit the unqualified approbation of the most fastidious epicures.

We ought, perhaps, to apologize for the apparent incongruity of connecting the "Toilet" with the "Kitchen;" but the receipts and suggestions comprised in the Second Part of the work before us, will not, we trust, be considered misplaced in a volume addressed exclusively to the ladies.

Many of the receipts are for articles in common use, but which, with proper directions, are prepared with greater economy and in a superior manner at home; the others are all original receipts, many of them extremely ancient, and given to us by a person who can vouch for their efficacy from personal experience and observation.

We must now conclude our preliminary remarks, but cannot take leave of our patient readers without availing ourselves of the opportunity our editorial capacity affords, to express our hope, that with all its faults and deficiencies " The Jewish Manual" may prove to them a useful assistant, and be fortunate enough to meet with their lenient, kind, and favourable consideration.

CONTENTS.

PART I.

INTRODUCTION.

CHAPTER V.

CHAPTER VI.

CHAPTER VII.

CHAPTER VIII.

CHAPTER IX.

CHAPTER X.

THE TOILETTE.

———

GLOSSARY.

Aspie, a term used for savoury jelly, in which cold poultry, meat, &c., is often served.

Bain-Marie. This is a large pan filled with boiling water, in which several saucepans can be placed when their contents are required to be kept hot without boiling—this is a useful article in a kitchen, where the manner in which sauces are prepared is considered deserving of attention.

Béchamel, a superior kind of white sauce, used in French cookery.

Blanquette, a kind of fricassee with a white sauce.

Bola-d'amour, a very rich and expensive Spanish confection.

Bolas, a kind of rich cake or pudding.

Cassereet, a sauce prepared from the cassada, a West Indian plant—it must be used with moderation.

Casserole, a name given to a crust formed of rice baked, and then filled with mince, fricassee, or fruit.

Chorissa, a sausage peculiar to the Jewish kitchen, of delicate and *piquante* flavour.

Consommé, is a term now used for stock—it is a clear strong broth, forming the basis of all soups, sauces, gravies, &c.

Croquettes and *Risoles*; preparations of forcemeat, formed into fancy shapes, and fried.

Croutons, sippets of bread or toast, to garnish hashes, salmis, &c., are so called.

Doce, a mixture of sugar with almonds *or* cocoa-nut.

Entrées. These are side-dishes, for the first course, consisting of cutlets, vol au vents, fricassees, fillets, sweetbreads, salmis, scallops, &c., &c.

Entremets. These are side-dishes for the second course; they comprise dressed vegetables, puddings, gateaux, pastries, fritters, creams, jellies, timbales, &c.

Farcie, a French term for forcemeat; it is a mixture of savoury ingredients, used for croquettes, balls, &c. Meat is by no means a necessary ingredient, although the English word might seem to imply the contrary.

Fondeaux, and Fondus, are savoury kinds of souflés.

Fricandeaux, a term for small well-trimmed pieces of meat, stewed in various ways.

Fricassee. This is a name used for delicate stews, when the articles are cut in pieces.

Fricandelles. These are very small fricandeaux, two or three of which are served on one dish, and they sometimes also are delicate, but highly-flavoured minces, formed into any approved shapes.

Flanks are large standing side-dishes.

Gateaux, is a kind of cake or pudding.

Hors d'œunes. These are light entrées in the first course; they are sometimes called *assiettes* volantes; they are handed during the first course; they comprise anchovies, fish salads, patties of various kinds, croquettes, risolles, maccaroni, &c.

Maigre, made without meat.

Matso, Passover cakes.

Miroton, a savoury preparation of veal or poultry, formed in a mould.

Nouilles, a kind of vermicelli paste.

Piqué, a French term used to expresss the process of larding. The French term is a preferable one, as it more clearly indicates what is meant,

Purée is a term given to a preparation of meat or vegetables, reduced to a pulp, and mixed with any kind of sauce, to the consistency of thick cream. *Purées* of vegetables are much used in modern cookery, to serve with cutlets, callops, &c.

Ramekin, a savoury and delicate preparation of cheese, generally served in fringed paper cases.

Releves, or *Removes*, are top and bottom dishes, which replace the soup and fish.

Salmis, a hash, only a superior kind, being more delicately seasoned, and usually made of cold poultry.

Souflés, a term applied to a a very light kind of pudding, made with some farinaceous substance, and generally replaces the roast of a second course.

Timbale, a shape of maccaroni or rice made in a mould.

Vol-au-vent. This is a sort of case, made of very rich puff paste, filled with delicate fricassee of fish, meat, or poultry, or richly stewed fruits.

Vélouté, an expensive white sauce.

OBSERVATIONS

FOR THE

USE OF THE COOK.

THE receipts we have given are capable of being varied and modified by an intelligent pains-taking cook, to suit the tastes of her employers.

Where *one* receipt has been thought sufficient to convey the necessary instruction for several dishes, &c., &c., it has not been repeated for each respectively, which plan will tend to facilitate her task.

We might, had we been inclined, have increased our collection considerably by so doing, but have decided, from our own experience, that it is preferable to give a limited number clearly and fully explained, as these will always serve as guides and models for others of the same kind.

The cook must remember it is not enough to have ascertained the ingredients and quantities requisite, but great care and attention must be paid to the manner of mixing them, and in watching their progress when mixed and submitted to the fire.

The management of the oven and the fire deserve attention, and cannot be regulated properly without practice and observation.

The art of seasoning is difficult and important.

Great judgment is required in blending the different spices or other condiments, so that a fine flavour is produced without the undue preponderance of either.

It is only in coarse cooking that the flavour of onions, pepper, garlic, nutmeg, and eschalot is permitted to prevail. As a general rule, salt should be used in moderation.

Sugar is an improvement in nearly all soups, sauces, and gravies; also with stewed vegetables, but of course must be used with discretion.

Ketchups, Soy, Harvey's sauce, &c., are used too indiscrimately by inferior cooks; it is better to leave them to be added at table by those who approve of their flavour.

Any thing that is required to be warmed up a second time, should be set in a basin placed in a *bain-marie*, or saucepan, filled with boiling water, but which must not be allowed to boil; or the article will become hardened and the sauce dried up.

To remove every particle of fat from the gravies of stews, &c., a piece of white blotting-paper should be laid on the surface, and the fat will adhere to it; this should be repeated two or three times.

It is important to keep saucepans well skimmed; the best prepared dish will be spoiled by neglect on this point.

The difference between good and bad cookery is particularly discernible in the preparation of forcemeats. A common cook is satistfied if she chops or minces the ingredients and moistens them with an egg scarcely beaten, but this is a very crude and imperfect method; they should be pounded together in a mortar until not a lump or fibre is perceptible. Further directions will be given in the proper place, but this is a rule which must be strictly attended to by those who wish to attain any excellence in this branch of their art.

Eggs for forcemeats, and for every description of sweet dishes, should be thoroughly beaten, and for the finer kinds should be passed through a sieve.

A trustworthy zealous servant must keep in mind, that waste and extravagance are no proofs of skill. On the contrary, GOOD COOKERY is by no means expensive, as it makes the most of every thing, and furnishes out of simple and economical materials, dishes which are at once palatable and elegant.

CHAPTER I.

Soups.

THIS is the basis of all kinds of soup and sauces.
Shin of beef or ox-cheek make excellent stock,
although good gravy-beef is sometimes preferred;
the bones should always be broken, and the meat
cut up, as the juices are better extracted; it is
advisable to put on, at first, but very little water,
and to add more when the first quantity is nearly
dried up. The time required for boiling depends
upon the quantity of meat; six pounds of meat
will take about five hours; if bones, the same
quantity will require double the time.

Gravy beef with a knuckle of veal makes a
fine and nutritious stock; the stock for white
soups should be prepared with veal or white

B

poultry. Very tolerable stock can be procured without purchasing meat expressly for the purpose, by boiling down bones and the trimmings of meat or poultry.

The liquor in which beef or mutton intended for the table has been boiled, will also, with small additions and skilful flavoring, make an excellent soup at a trifling expense.

To thicken soups, mix a little potatoe-flour, ground rice, or pounded vermicelli, in a little water, till perfectly smooth; add a little of the soup to it in a cup, until sufficiently thin, then pour it into the rest and boil it up, to prevent the raw taste it would otherwise have; the presence of the above ingredients should not be discovered, and judgment and care are therefore requisite.

If colouring is necessary, a crust of bread stewed in the stock will give a fine brown, or the common browning may be used; it is made in the following manner:

Put one pound of coarse brown sugar in a stew-pan with a lump of clarified suet; when it begins to froth, pour in a wine-glass of port wine, half an ounce of black pepper, a little mace, four spoonsful of ketchup or Harvey's sauce, a little salt, and the peel of a lemon grated; boil all together, let it grow cold, when it must be skimmed and bottled for use.

It may also be prepared as required, by putting a small piece of clarified fat with one ounce of coarse sugar, in an iron spoon, melting them together, and stirring in a little ketchup and pepper.

When good stock or consommé is prepared, it is very easy to form it into any kind of soup or sauce that may be required.

GRAVY SOUP.

Take about three quarts of any strong stock, seasoned with a bunch of sweet herbs, a carrot, turnip, and a head of celery, which must not be served in the soup. Vermicelli, maccaroni, or thin slices of carrot and small sippets of fried bread cut in fancy shapes, are usually served in this soup.

MOCK TURTLE.

Half boil a well-cleaned calf's head, then cut off all the meat in small square pieces, and break the bones; return it to the stew-pan, with some good stock made of beef and veal; dredge in flour, add fried shalot, pepper, parsley, tarragon, a little mushroom ketchup, and a pint of white wine; simmer gently until the meat is perfectly soft and tender. Balls of force-meat, and egg-balls, should be put in a short time before serving; the juice of a lemon is considered an improvement.

MULIGATAWNY SOUP.

Take two chickens, cut them up small, as if for fricassee, flour them well, put them in a saucepan with four onions shred, a piece of clarified fat, pepper, salt, and two table spoonsful of curry powder; let it simmer for an hour, then add three quarts of strong beef gravy, and let it continue simmering for another hour; before sent to table the juice of a lemon should be stirred in it; some persons approve of a little rice being boiled with the stock, and a pinch of saffron is also sometimes added.

ENGLISH MULIGATAWNY.

Take a knuckle of veal, stew it till half done, then cut off the greatest part of the meat, and continue to stew down the bone in the stock, the meat must be cut into small pieces and fried with six onions thinly sliced, and a table spoonful of curry powder, a desert spoonful of cayenne pepper and salt, add the stock and let the whole gently simmer for nearly an hour, flavouring it with a little Harvey's sauce and lemon pickle.

SOUP A LA JULIENNE.

Take a variety of vegetables: such as celery, carrots, turnips, leeks, cauliflower, lettuce, and onions, cut them in shreds of small size, place them in a stew-pan with a little fine salad oil, stew them gently over the fire, adding weak broth from time to time; toast a few slices of bread and cut them into pieces the size and shape of shillings and crowns, soak them in the remainder of the broth, and when the vegetables are well done add all together and let it simmer for a few minutes; a lump of white sugar, with pepper and salt are sufficient seasoning.

SOUPE A LA TURQUE.

Make a good gravy from shin of beef, and cut up very small various sorts of vegetables of whatever may be in season, add spices, pepper, and salt; when it is all stewed well down together, set it to cool and take off the fat, then place it again on the fire to boil, and add to two quarts of soup, one quarter of a pound of rice, beat two yolks of eggs with a little of the stock, and when the rice is quite tender, stir them into the soup, taking the precaution not to let the soup boil, and to stir always the same way.

PEPPER POT.

Cut small pieces of any vegetables, and add pieces of smoked or salt beef, and also of any cold poultry, roast beef or mutton, stew all these together in two or three quarts of water, according to the quantity of meat, &c. It must be seasoned highly with whole peppers, allspice, mace, Jamaica pickles, and salt ; it must be thoroughly stewed, and served, without straining, in a tureen.

POTATOE SOUP.

Grate a pound of fine potatoes in two quarts of water, add to it the trimmings of any meat, amounting to about a pound in quantity, a cup of rice, a few sweet herbs, and a head of celery, stew well till the liquor is considerably reduced, then strain it through a sieve ; if, when strained, it is too thin and watery, add a little thickening ; it should be flavoured only with white pepper and salt.

SOUP CRESSY.

Grate six carrots, and chop some onions with a lettuce, adding a few sweet herbs, put them all into a stewpan, with enough of good broth to moisten the whole, adding occasionally the remainder; when nearly done, put in the crumb of a French roll, and when soaked, strain the whole through a sieve, and serve hot in a tureen.

CARROT SOUP.

Take a dozen carrots scraped clean, rasp them, but do not use the core, two heads of celery, two onions thinly sliced, season to taste, and pour over a good stock, say about two quarts, boil it, then pass it through a sieve; it should be of the thickness of cream, return it to the saucepan, boil it up and squeeze in a little lemon juice, or add a little vinegar.

PALESTINE SOUP.

Stew a knuckle of veal, and a calf's foot, and one pound of *chorissa*, and a large fowl, in four quarts of water, add a piece of fresh lemon peel, six Jerusalem artichokes, a bunch of sweet herbs, a little salt and white pepper, and a little nutmeg, and a blade of mace; when the fowl is thoroughly done, remove the white parts to prepare for thickening, and let the rest continue stewing till the stock is sufficiently strong, the white parts of the fowl must be pounded and sprinkled with flower or ground rice, and stirred in the soup after it has been strained, until it thickens.

A SIMPLE WHITE SOUP.

Break a knuckle of veal, place it in a stewpan, also a piece of *chorissa*, a carrot, two onions, three or four turnips, and a blade of mace, pour over two or three quarts of water or weak broth, season with salt, a sprig of parsley, and whole white pepper; when sufficiently boiled, skim and strain it, and thicken with pounded vermicelli.

VERMICELLI SOUP.

Make a fine strong stock from the shin of beef, or any other part preferred, and add, a short time before serving, a handful of vermicelli, which should be broken, so that it may be in pieces of convenient length, the stock should be more or less flavoured with vegetables, and herbs, according to taste.

MATSO SOUP.

Boil down half a shin of beef, four pounds of gravy beef, and a calf's foot may be added, if approved, in three or four quarts of water; season with celery, carrots, turnips, pepper and

salt, and a bunch of sweet herbs; let the whole
stew gently for eight hours, then strain and
let it stand to get cold, when the fat must be
removed, then return it to the saucepan to warm
up. Ten minutes before serving, throw in the
balls, from which the soup takes its name, and
which are made in the following manner:

Take half a pound of *matso* flour, two ounces
of chopped suet, season with a little pepper,
salt, ginger, and nutmeg; mix with this, four
beaten eggs, and make it into a paste, a small
onion shred and browned in a desert spoonful
of oil is sometimes added; the paste should be
made into rather large balls, and care should
be taken to make them very light.

TOMATA SOUP.

Take a dozen unpealed tomatas, with a bit
of clarified suet, or a little sweet oil, and a
small Spanish onion; sprinkle with flour, and
season with salt and cayenne pepper, and boil
them in a little gravy or water; it must be
stirred to prevent burning, then pass it through
a sieve, and thin it with rich stock to the consistency of winter pea-soup; flavour it with

lemon juice, according to taste, after it has
been warmed up and ready for serving.

ALMONDEGOS SOUP: A SUPERIOR WHITE SOUP.

Put a knuckle of veal and a calf's foot into
two quarts of water, with a blade of mace and
a bunch of sweet herbs, a turnip, a little white
pepper, and salt; when sufficiently done, strain
and skim it, and add balls of forced meat, and
egg balls. A quarter of an hour before serving
beat up the yolks of four eggs with a desert
spoonful of lemon juice, and three ounces of
sweet almonds blanched and beaten with a spoonful of powdered white sugar. This mixture is
to be stirred into the soup till it thickens,
taking care to prevent its curdling.

A FINE VEGETABLE OR FRENCH SOUP.

Take two quarts of strong stock made of gravy
beef, add to this, carrots, turnips, leek, celery,
brocoli, peas and French beans, all cut as small
as possible, add a few lumps of white sugar, pepper, and salt, let it simmer till the vegetables are

perfectly soft, and throw in a few force-meat balls.

___

ASPARAGUS SOUP.

Take eight pounds of gravy beef, with five pints of water, a few sweet herbs, and an onion shred, with a little pepper and salt; when the strength of the meat is sufficiently extracted, strain off the soup, and add to it a bundle of asparagus, cut small, with a little chopped parsley and mint; the asparagus should be thoroughly done. A few minutes before serving, throw in some fried bread cut up the size of dice; pound a little spinach to a pulp, and squeeze it through a cloth, stir about a tea-cup full of this essence into the soup, let it boil up after to prevent a raw taste.

___

SOUP MAIGRE.

Chop three lettuces, a large handful of spinach, a little chervil, a head of celery, two or three carrots, and four onions, put them on the fire with half a pound of butter, and let them fry till slightly browned, season with a little salt, sifted white sugar, and white pepper, stew all gently in five pints of boiling water for about two hours and a half, and just before serving the soup, thicken it with the beaten yolks of four eggs, mixed first with a little of the soup, and then stirred into the remainder.

SUMMER PEA SOUP.

Take a peck of peas, separate the old from the young, boil the former till they are quite tender in good stock, then pass them through a sieve, and return them to the stock, add the young peas, a little chopped lettuce, small pieces of cucumber fried to a light brown, a little bit of mint, pepper, and salt; two or three lumps of sugar give a fine flavor.

WINTER PEA SOUP.

Soak a quart of white peas in water, boil them till soft, in as much water as will cover them, pass them through a sieve, and add them to any broth that may be ready, a little piece of *chorissa* or smoked beef will improve the flavour; this soup should be served with mint and fried bread.

———

GIBLET SOUP.

Add to a fine strong well-seasoned beef stock, of about three quarts, two sets of giblets, which should be previously stewed separately in one quart of water (the gizzards require scalding for some time before they are put in with the rest); white pepper, salt, and the rind of lemon should season them; when they are tender, add them with their gravy to the stock, and boil for about ten minutes together, then stir in a glass of white wine, a table spoonful of mushroom ketchup, and the juice of half a lemon; it will require to be thickened with a little flour browned; the giblets are served in the soup.

———

BARLEY SOUP.

Put in a stew-pan, a knuckle of mutton, or four pounds of the neck, with three quarts of water, boil it gently and keep it well skimmed; a sprig of parsley, a couple of sliced turnips, a carrot, an onion or more, if approved, with a little white pepper and salt, are sufficient seasoning, a breakfast cup full of barley should be scalded and put in the stew-pan with the meat, if when done, the soup is thin and watery, a little prepared barley, mixed smoothly, should be stirred in.

———

SOUP DE POISSON, OR FISH SOUP.

Make a good stock, by simmering a cod's-head in water, enough to cover the fish; season it with pepper and salt, mace, celery, parsley, and a few sweet herbs, with two or three onions, when sufficiently done, strain it, and add cutlets of fish prepared in the following manner: cut very small, well-trimmed cutlets from any fish, sole or brill are perhaps best suited; stew them in equal quantities of water and wine, but not more than will cover them, with a large lump of butter, and the juice of a lemon; when they have stewed gently for about fifteen or twenty minutes, add them to the soup, which thicken with cream and flour, serve the soup with the cutlets in a tureen; force-meat balls of cod's liver are sometimes added.

———

OX TAIL SOUP.

Have two well cleaned tails and a neat's foot, cut them in small joints and soak them in water, put them in a stew-pan with a large piece of clarified suet or fat, and let them simmer for ten minutes, then put to them between three and four quarts of cold water, four onions, a bunch of sweet herbs, a carrot, a turnip, a head of celery, and season with whole pepper, allspice, two or three cloves, and salt; let it stew till the meat is tender enough to leave the bones, then remove it from them, as the bones are unsightly in the soup; thicken if necessary with browned flour, and just before serving, add a glass or more of port wine, and a little mushroom ketchup.

CHAPTER II.

Sauces.

A RICH BROWN GRAVY.

Take a little good beef consommé, or stock, a small piece of smoked beef, or *chorissa*, a lemon sliced, some chopped shalots, a couple of onions shred, a bay leaf, two or three cloves, and a little oil; simmer gently, and add a little minced parsley, and a few chopped mushrooms : skim and strain.

SAUCE PIQUANTE.

The above may be rendered a Sauce Piquante by substituting a little vinegar, whole capers, allspice, and thyme, instead of the smoked beef

c

and lemon; a few onions and piccalilli chopped finely, is a great addition when required to be very piquante.

A sauce like the above is very good to serve with beef that has been boiled for broth.

A GOOD GRAVY FOR ROAST FOWLS.

Take a little stock, squeeze in the juice of a lemon, add a little mushroom powder, cayenne pepper and salt; thicken with flour.

ANOTHER EXCELLENT RECEIPT.

Chop some mushrooms, young and fresh, salt them, and put them into a saucepan with a little gravy, made of the trimmings of the fowl, or of veal, a blade of mace, a little grated lemon peel, the juice of one lemon; thicken with flour, and when ready to serve, stir in a table-spoonful of white wine.

EGG SAUCE:
A FINE WHITE SAUCE FOR BOILED CHICKENS, TURKEYS, OR WHITE FRICASSEES.

Beat up the yolks of four eggs with the juice of a fine lemon, a tea-spoonful of flour, and a little cold water, mix well together, and set it on the fire to thicken, stirring it to prevent curdling. This sauce will be found excellent, if not superior, in many cases where English cooks use melted butter. If capers are substituted for the lemon juice, this sauce will be found excellent for boiled lamb or mutton.

CELERY SAUCE.

Cut in small pieces from about four to five heads of celery, which if not very young must be peeled, simmer it till tender in half a pint of veal gravy, if intended for white sauce, then add a spoonful of flour, the yolks of three eggs, white pepper, salt, and the juice of one lemon, these should be previously mixed together with a little water till perfectly smooth and thin, and be stirred in with the sauce; cream, instead of eggs, is used in English kitchens.

TOMATO SAUCE.

Skin a dozen fine tomatos, set them on the fire in a little water or gravy, beat them up with

a little vinegar, lemon juice, cayenne pepper,
and salt ; some persons like the yolk of an egg,
well beaten added. Strain or not, as may be
preferred.

GRAVY FOR A FOWL,
WHEN THERE IS NO STOCK TO MAKE IT WITH.

Take the feet, wash them, cut them small,
also the neck and gizzard; season them with
pepper and salt, onion, and parsley, let them simmer gently for some time, in about a breakfast-
cup of water, then strain, thicken with flour,
and add a little browning, and if liked, a small
quantity of any store sauce at hand, and it will
prove an excellent sauce.

SAVOURY JELLY,
FOR COLD PIES, OR TO GARNISH COLD POULTRY.

Have a bare knuckle of veal, and a calf's foot
or cow heel; put it into a stew-pan with a thick
slice of smoked beef, a few herbs, a blade of
mace, two or three onions, a little lemon peel,
pepper and salt, and three or four pints of

water (the French add a little tarragon vinegar). When it boils skim it, and when cold, if
not clear, boil it a few minutes with the white
and shell of an egg, and pass it through a jelly
bag, this jelly with the juice of two or three
lemons, and poured into a mould, in which are
put the yolks of eggs boiled hard, forms a pretty
supper dish.

A FINE SAUCE FOR STEAKS.

Throw into a saucepan a piece of fat the size
of an egg, with two or three onions sliced, let
them brown; add a little gravy, flour, a little
vinegar, a spoonful of mustard, and a little
cayenne pepper, boil it and serve with the
steaks.

A FISH SAUCE WITHOUT BUTTER.

Put on, in a small saucepan, a cup of water,
well flavored with vinegar, an onion chopped
fine, a little rasped horse-radish, pepper, and
two or three cloves, and a couple of anchovies
cut small, when it has boiled, stir carefully in
the beaten yolks of two eggs, and let it thicken,
until of the consistency of melted butter.

A FINE FISH SAUCE.

One teacup full of walnut pickle, the same of mushroom ditto, three anchovies pounded, one clove of garlic pounded, half a tea-spoonful of cayenne pepper, all mixed well together, and bottled for use.

——

A NICE SAUCE TO THROW OVER BROILED MEATS.

Beat up a little salad-oil with a table-spoonful of vinegar, mustard, pepper and salt, and then stir in the yolk of an egg; this sauce should be highly seasoned. A sauce of this description is sometimes used to baste mutton while roasting, the meat should be scored in different places to allow the sauce to penetrate.

——

SAUCE FOR DUCKS.

A little good gravy, with a glass of port wine, the juice of a lemon, highly seasoned with cayenne pepper.

——

BREAD SAUCE.

Take a large onion and boil it, with a little pepper till quite soft, in milk, then take it out, and pour the milk over grated stale bread, then boil it up with a piece of butter, and dredge it with flour; it should be well beaten up with a silver fork.

The above can be made without butter or milk: take a large onion, slice it thin, put it into a little veal gravy, add grated bread, pepper, &c., and the yolk and white of an egg well beaten.

APPLE SAUCE FOR GOOSE.

Slice some apples, put them in a little water to simmer till soft, beat them to a pulp; some consider a little powdered sugar an improvement, but as the acid of the apples is reckoned a corrective to the richness of the goose, it is usually preferred without.

MINT SAUCE.

Mix vinegar with brown sugar, let it stand about an hour, then add chopped mint, and stir together.

ONION SAUCE.

Slice finely, and brown in a little oil, two or three onions; put them in a little beef gravy, and add cayenne pepper, salt, and the juice of a lemon. This is a nice sauce for steaks.

OILED BUTTER.

Put some good butter into a cup or jar, and place it before the fire till it becomes an oil, then pour it off, so that all sediment may be avoided.

TO DRAW GOOD GRAVY.

Cut some gravy beef into small pieces, put them in a jar, and set it in a saucepan of cold water to boil gently for seven or eight hours, adding, from time to time, more water as the original quantity boils away. The gravy thus made will be the essence of the meat, and in cases where nutriment is required in the smallest compass, will be of great service. Soups are stronger when the meat is cut, and gravy drawn before water is added.

TRUFFLE SAUCE.

Peel and slice as many truffles as required, simmer them gently with a little butter, when they are tender, add to them good white or brown consommé, lemon juice, pepper, salt, nutmeg, and a very little white wine.

MUSHROOM SAUCE.

Take about a pint of fine young button mushrooms, let them stew gently in a white veal gravy seasoned with salt, pepper, a blade of mace, and if approved, the grated peel of half a lemon, it should be thickened with flour and the yolk of an egg stirred in it, just before serving; English cooks add cream to this sauce.

SWEET SAUCE.

The usual way of making sauces for puddings, is by adding sugar to melted butter, or thin egg sauce, flavoring it with white wine, brandy, lemon peel, or any other flavor approved of.

MELTED BUTTER.

Although this sauce is one of the most simple, it is very rarely that it is well made. Mix with four ounces of butter, a desert spoonful of

flour, when well mixed, add three table spoonsful of water, put it into a clean saucepan kept
for the purpose, and stir it carefully one way
till it boils; white sauce to throw over vegetables served on toast, is made in the same way,
only putting milk and water, instead of water
only.

SAUCE WITHOUT BUTTER FOR BOILED PUDDINGS.

Mix a table-spoonful of flour, with two of
water, add a little wine, lemon peel grated, a
small bit of clarified suet, of the size of a walnut, grated nutmeg, and sugar, put on in a
saucepan, stirring one way, and adding water if
too thick, lemon juice, or essence of noyeau,
or almonds may be substituted to vary the
flavour.

SAUCE ROBERT FOR STEAKS.

Chop up some onions, throw them into a
saucepan with a bit of clarified fat, let them fry
till brown, then add pepper, salt, a little gravy,
mustard, lemon juice, and vinegar; boil it all,
and pour over the steaks.

CAPER SAUCE.

This is merely melted butter with a few pickled capers simmered in it, or they may be put into a sauce made of broth thickened with egg, and a little flour.

SAVORY HERB POWDER.

It is useful to select a variety of herbs, so that they may always be at hand for use: the following are considered to be an excellent selection, parsley, savory, thyme, sweet majoram, shalot, chervil, and sage, in equal quantities; dry these in the oven, pound them finely and keep them in bottles well stopped.

SEASONING FOR DUCKS AND GEESE.

Mix chopped onion with an equal quantity of chopped sage, three times as much grated stale bread, a little shred suet, pepper, salt, and a beaten egg to bind it, this is generally used for geese and ducks, the onions are sometimes boiled first to render them less strong.

ENGLISH EGG SAUCE.

Boil two eggs hard, chop them finely, and warm them up in finely made melted butter, add a little white pepper, salt, a blade of mace, and a very small quantity of nutmeg.

SAUCE A LA TARTARE.

Mix the yolk of an egg with oil, vinegar, chopped parsley, mustard, pepper, and salt; a spoonful of paté de diable or French mustard, renders the sauce more piquante.

A FINE SAUCE FOR ROAST MUTTON.

Mix a little port wine in some gravy, two table-spoonfuls of vinegar, one of oil, a shalot minced, and a spoonful of mustard, just before the mutton is served, pour the sauce over it, then sprinkle it with fried bread crumbs, and then again baste the meat with the sauce; this is a fine addition to the mutton.

ASPARAGUS SAUCE, TO SERVE WITH LAMB CHOPS.

Cut some asparagus, or sprew, into half inch lengths, wash them, and throw them into half a pint of gravy made from beef, veal, or mutton thickened, and seasoned with salt, white pepper, and a lump of white sugar, the chops should be delicately fried and the sauce served in the centre of the dish.

BROWN CUCUMBER SAUCE.

Peel and cut in thick slices, one or more fresh cucumbers, fry them until brown in a little butter, or clarified fat, then add to them a little strong beef gravy, pepper, salt, and a spoonful of vinegar; some cooks add a chopped onion browned with the cucumbers.

WHITE CUCUMBER SAUCE.

Take out the seeds of some fresh young cucumbers, quarter them, and cut them into pieces of two inch lengths, let them lay for an hour in vinegar and water, then simmer them till thoroughly soft, in a veal broth seasoned with pepper, salt, and a little lemon juice; when ready for serving, pour off the gravy and thicken it with the yolks of a couple of eggs stirred in, add it to the saucepan; warm up, taking care that it does not curdle.

BROWNED FLOUR FOR MAKING SOUPS AND GRAVIES DARK AND THICK.

Spread flour on a tin, and place it in a Dutch oven before the fire, or in a gentle oven till it browns; it must often be turned, that the flour may be equally coloured throughout. A small quantity of this prepared and laid by for use, will be found useful.

———

BROWNED BREAD CRUMBS.

Grate into fine crumbs, about five or six ounces of stale bread, and brown them in a gentle oven or before the fire ; this is a more delicate way of browning them than by frying.

———

CRISPED PARSLEY.

Wash and drain a handful of fresh young sprigs of parsley, dry them with a cloth, place them before the fire on a dish, turn them frequently, and they will be perfectly crisp in ten minutes.

———

FRIED PARSLEY.

When the parsley is prepared as above, fry it in butter or clarified suet, then drain it on a cloth placed before the fire.

BREAD CRUMBS FOR FRYING.

Cut slices of bread without crust, and dry them gradually in a cool oven till quite dry and crisp, then roll them into fine crumbs, and put them in a jar for use.

SPINACH GREEN.

Pound to a pulp in a mortar a handful of spinach, and squeeze it through a hair sieve; then put it into a cup or jar, and place it in a basin of hot water for a few minutes, or it may be allowed to simmer on the fire; a little of this stirred into spring soups, improve their appearance.

VELOUTÉ, BECHAMEL.

These preparations are so frequently mentioned in modern cookery, that we shall give the receipts for them, although they are not appropriate for the Jewish kitchen. Velouté is a fine white sauce, made by reducing a certain quantity of well-flavoured consommé or stock, over a charcoal fire, and mixing it with boiling cream, stirring it carefully till it thickens.

Béchamel is another sort of fine white stock, thickened with cream, there is more flavouring in this than the former, the stock is made of veal, with some of the smoked meats used in English kitchens, butter, mace, onion, mushrooms, bay leaf, nutmeg, and a little salt. An excellent substitute for these sauces can in Jewish kitchens be made in the following way:

Take some veal broth flavored with smoked beef, and the above named seasonings, then beat up two or three yolks of eggs, with a little of the stock and a spoonful of potatoe flour, stir this into the broth, until it thickens, it will not be quite as white, but will be excellent.

———

FORCEMEAT OR FARCIE.

Under this head is included the various preparations used for balls, tisoles, fritters, and

stuffings for poultry and veal, it is a branch of
cooking which requires great care and judgment, the proportions should be so blended as
to produce a delicate, yet savoury flavor, without
allowing any particular herb or spice to predo-
minate.

The ingredients should always be pounded
well together in a mortar, not merely chopped
and moistened with egg, as is usually done by
inexperienced cooks; forcemeat can be served
in a variety of forms, and is so useful a resource,
that it well repays the attention it requires.

A SUPERIOR FORCEMEAT FOR RISOLLES, FRITTERS, AND SAVORY MEAT BALLS.

Scrape half a pound of the fat of smoked
beef, and a pound of lean veal, free from skin,
vein, or sinew, pound it finely in a mortar with
chopped mushrooms, a little minced parsley, salt
and pepper, and grated lemon peel, then have
ready the crumb of two French rolls soaked in
good gravy, press out the moisture, and add the
crumb to the meat with three beaten eggs; if
the forcemeat is required to be very highly

D

flavored, the gravy in which the rolls are soaked should be seasoned with mushroom powder; a spoonful of ketchup, a bay leaf, an onion, pepper, salt, and lemon juice, add this panada to the pounded meat and eggs, form the mixture into any form required, and either fry or warm in gravy, according to the dish for which it is intended.

Any cold meats pounded, seasoned, and made according to the above method are excellent; the seasoning can be varied, or rendered simpler if required.

COMMON VEAL STUFFING.

Have equal quantities of finely shred suet and grated crumbs of bread, add chopped sweet herbs, grated lemon peel, pepper, and salt, pound it in a mortar; this is also used for white poultry, with the addition of a little grated smoked beef, or a piece of the root of a tongue pounded and mixed with the above ingredients.

FISH FORCEMEAT.

Chop finely any kind of fish, that which has been already dressed will answer the purpose, then pound it in a mortar with a couple of anchovies, or a little anchovy essence, the yolk of a hard boiled egg, a little butter, parsley or any other herb which may be approved, grated lemon peel, and a little of the juice, then add a little bread previously soaked, and mix the whole into a paste, and form into balls, or use for stuffing, &c.

The liver or roe of fish is well suited to add to the fish, as it is rich and delicate.

FORCEMEAT FOR DRESSING FISH FILLETS.

Pound finely anchovies, grated bread, chopped parsley, and the yolk of a hard boiled egg, add grated lemon peel, a little lemon juice, pepper and salt, and make into a paste with two eggs.

FORCEMEAT FOR DRESSING CUTLETS, ETC.

Add to grated stale bread, an equal quantity of chopped parsley, season it well, and mix it with clarified suet, then brush the cutlets with beaten yolks of eggs, lay on the mixture thickly with a knife, and sprinkle over with dry and fine bread crumbs.

_____

EGG BALLS.

Beat the hard yolks of eggs in a mortar, make it into a paste with the yolk of a raw egg, form the paste into very small balls, and throw them into boiling water for a minute or so, to harden them.

_____

PREPARATION FOR CUTLETS OF FOWL OR VEAL.

Make a smooth batter of flour, and a little salad oil, and two eggs, a little white pepper, salt, and nutmeg, turn the cutlets well in this mixture, and fry a light brown, garnish with slices of lemon, and crisped parsley, this is done by putting in the parsley after the cutlets have been fried, it will speedily crisp; it should then be drained, to prevent its being greasy.

CHAPTER III.

Fish.

———

PRELIMINARY REMARKS.

WHEN fish is to be boiled, it should be rubbed lightly over with salt, and set on the fire in a saucepan or fish-kettle sufficiently large, in hard cold water, with a little salt, a spoonful or two of vinegar is sometimes added, which has the effect of increasing its firmness.

Fish for broiling should be rubbed over with vinegar, well dried in a cloth and floured. The fire must be clear and free from smoke, the grid-iron made quite hot, and the bars buttered before the fish is put on it. Fish to be fried should be rubbed in with salt, dried, rolled in a cloth, and placed for a few minutes before the fire previous to being put in the pan.

FISH FRIED IN OIL.

Soles, plaice, or salmon, are the best kinds of
fish to dress in this manner, although various
other sorts are frequently used.   When prepared
by salting or drying, as above directed, have a
dish ready with beaten eggs, turn the fish well
over in them, and sprinkle it freely with flour,
so that the fish may be covered entirely with it,
then place it in a pan with a good quantity of
the best frying oil at boiling heat; fry the fish
in it gently, till of a fine equal brown colour,
when done, it should be placed on a cloth before
the fire for the oil to drain off; great care should
be observed that the oil should have ceased to
bubble when the fish is put in, otherwise it will
be greasy; the oil will serve for two or three
times if strained off and poured into a jar.   Fish
prepared in this way is usually served cold.

FRIED SOLES IN THE ENGLISH WAY.

Prepare the soles as directed in the last receipt, brush them over with egg, dredge them
with stale bread crumbs, and fry in boiling

butter; this method is preferable when required
to be served hot.

ESCOBECHE.

Take some cold fried fish, place it in a deep
pan, then boil half a pint of vinegar with two
table spoonsful of water, and one of oil, a little
grated ginger, allspice, cayenne pepper, two bay
leaves, a little salt, and a table spoonful of lemon
juice, with sliced onions; when boiling, pour it
over the fish, cover the pan, and let it stand
twenty-four hours before serving.

FISH STEWED WHITE.

Put an onion, finely chopped, into a stew-pan,
with a little oil, till the onion becomes brown,
then add half a pint of water, and place the fish
in the stew-pan, seasoning with pepper, salt,
mace, ground allspice, nutmeg, and ginger; let
it stew gently till the fish is done, then prepare
the beaten yolks of four eggs, with the juice of
two lemons, and a tea spoonful of flour, a table
spoonful of cold water, and a little saffron, mix
well in a cup, and pour it into the stew-pan,

stirring it carefully one way until it thickens. Balls should be thrown in about twenty minutes before serving; they are made in the following way: take a little of the fish, the liver, and roe, if there is any, beat it up finely with chopped parsley, and spread warmed butter, crumbs of bread, and seasoning according to taste; form this into a paste with eggs, and make it into balls of a moderate size; this is a very nice dish when cold; garnish with sliced lemon and parsley.

AN EXCELLENT RECEIPT FOR STEWED FISH IN THE DUTCH FASHION.

Take three or four parsley roots, cut them into pieces, slice several onions and boil in a pint of water till tender, season with lemon juice, vinegar, saffron, pepper, salt, and mace, then add the fish, and let it stew till nearly finished, when remove it, and thicken the gravy with a little flour and butter, and the yolk of one egg, then return the fish to the stew-pan, with balls made as directed in the preceding receipt, and boil up.

FISH STEWED BROWN.

Fry some fish of a light brown, either soles, slices of salmon, halibut, or plaice, let an onion brown in a little oil, add to it a cup of water, a little mushroom ketchup or powder, cayenne pepper, salt, nutmeg, and lemon juice, put the fish into a stew-pan with the above mixture, and simmer gently till done, then take out the fish and thicken the gravy with a little browned flour, and stir in a glass of port wine; a few truffles, or mushrooms, are an improvement.

WATER SOUCHY.

Take a portion of the fish intended to be dressed, and stew it down with three pints of water, parsley roots, and chopped parsley, and then pulp them through a sieve, then add the rest of the fish, with pepper, salt, and seasoning; and serve in a deep dish.

A SUPERIOR RECEIPT FOR STEWED CARP.

Clean the fish thoroughly, put it into a sauce-pan, with a strong rich gravy, season with onion, parsley roots, allspice, nutmegs, beaten cloves, and ginger, let it stew very gently till nearly done, then mix port wine and vinegar in equal quantities, coarse brown sugar and lemon juice, a little flour, with some of the gravy from the saucepan, mix well and pour over the fish, let it boil till the gravy thickens. Pike is excellent stewed in this manner.

FILLETS OF FISH.

Fillets of salmon, soles, &c., fried of a delicate brown according to the receipt already given, and served with a fine gravy is a very nice dish.

If required to be very savory, make a fish force-meat, and lay it thickly on the fish before frying ; fillets dressed in this way are usually arranged round the dish, and served with a sauce made of good stock, thickened and seasoned with cayenne pepper, lemon juice, and mush-room essence ; piccalilli are sometimes added cut small.

BAKED HADDOCK.

Carefully clean a fresh haddock, and fill it with a fine forcemeat, and sew it in securely; give the fish a dredging of flour, and pour on warmed butter, sprinkle it with pepper and salt, and set it to bake in a Dutch-oven before the fire, basting it, from time to time, with butter warmed, and capers; it should be of a rich dark brown, and it is as well to dredge two or three times with flour while at the fire, the continual bastings will produce sufficient sauce to serve with it without any other being added.

Mackarel and whiting prepared in this manner are excellent, the latter should be covered with a layer of bread crumbs, and arranged in a ring, and the forcemeat, instead of stuffing them, should be formed into small balls, and served in the dish as a garnish.

The forcemeat must be made as for veal stuffing, with the addition of a couple of minced anchovies, cayenne pepper, and butter instead of suet.

A NICE WAY OF DRESSING RED HERRINGS.

Open them, cut off the tails and heads, soak them ·in hot water for an hour, then wipe them dry; mix with warmed butter one beaten egg, pour this over the herrings, sprinkle with bread crumbs, flour, and white pepper, broil them and serve them very hot.

―――――

BAKED MACKAREL WITH VINEGAR.

Cut off the heads and tails, open and clean them, lay them in a deep pan with a few bay leaves, whole pepper, half a tea-spoonful of cloves, and a whole spoonful of allspice, pour over equal quantities of vinegar and water, and bake for an hour and a half, in a gentle oven; herrings and sprats are also dressed according to this receipt.

―――――

FISH SALAD.

Cut in small pieces any cold dressed fish, turbot or salmon are the best suited; mix it with half a pint of small salad, and a lettuce cut small, two onions boiled till tender and mild, and a few truffles thinly sliced; pour over a fine salad mixture, and arrange it into a shape, high in the centre, and garnish with hard eggs cut in slices; a little cucumber mixed with the salad is an improvement. The mixture may either be a

common salad mixture, or made as follows: take
the yolks of three hard boiled eggs, with a
spoonful of mustard, and a little salt, mix these
with a cup of cream, and four table-spoonsful
of vinegar, the different ingredients should be
added carefully and worked together smoothly,
the whites of the eggs may be trimmed and
placed in small heaps round the dish as a
garnish.

IMPANADA.

Cut in small pieces halibut, plaice, or soles,
place them in a deep dish in alternate layers,
with slices of potatoes and dumplings made of
short-crust paste, sweetened with brown sugar,
season well with small pickles, peppers, gerkins,
or West India pickles; throw over a little
water and butter warmed, and bake it thoroughly.

WHITE BAIT.

This is such a delicate fish that there are few
cooks who attempt to dress it without spoiling it;
they should not be touched but thrown from the

dish into a cloth with a handful of flour; shake them lightly, but enough to cover them well with the flour, then turn them into a sieve expressly for bait to free them from too great a quantity of the flour, then throw the fish into a pan with plenty of boiling butter, they must remain but an instant, for they are considered spoilt if they become the least brown; they should be placed lightly on the dish piled up high in the centre, brown bread and butter is always served with them; when devilled they are also excellent, and are permitted to become brown; they are then sprinkled with cayenne pepper, and a little salt, and served with lemon juice.

This receipt was given by a cook who dressed white bait to perfection.

A DUTCH FRICANDELLE.

Take two pounds of dressed fish, remove the skin and bones, cut in small pieces with two or three anchovies, and season well, soak the crumb of a French roll in milk, beat it up with the fish and three eggs: butter a mould, sprinkle

it with raspings, place in the fish and bake it;
when done, turn out and serve either dry or
with anchovy sauce ; if served dry, finely grated
crumbs of bread should be sprinkled thickly
over it, and it should be placed for a few
minutes before the fire to brown.

FISH FRITTERS.

Make a force-meat of any cold fish, form
it into thin cakes, and fry of a light brown, or
enclose them first in thin paste and then fry
them. The roes of fish or the livers are particularly nice prepared in this way.

FISH OMELET.

Shred finely any cold fish, season it, and mix
with beaten eggs ; make it into a paste, fry in
thin cakes like pancakes, and serve hot on a
napkin ; there should be plenty of boiling
butter in the pan, as they should be moist and
rich ; there should be more eggs in the preparation for omelets than for fritters.

SCALLOPED FISH.

Take any dressed fish, break it in small pieces,
put it into tin scallops, with a few crumbs of
bread, a good piece of butter, a little cream if
approved, white pepper, salt, and nutmeg; bake
in an oven for ten minutes, or brown before the
fire; two or three mushrooms mixed, or an
anchovy will be found an improvement.

ANOTHER WAY.

Break the fish into pieces, pour over the
beaten yolk of an egg, sprinkle with pepper and
salt, strew with bread crumbs, chopped parsley,
and grated lemon peel, and squeeze in the juice
of lemon, drop over a little warmed butter, and
brown before the fire.

CHAPTER IV.

DIRECTIONS FOR VARIOUS WAYS OF DRESSING

Meat and Poultry.

INTRODUCTORY REMARKS.

Boiling is the most simple manner of cooking, the great art in this process is to boil the article sufficiently, without its being overdone, the necessity of slow boiling cannot be too strongly impressed upon the cook, as the contrary, renders it hard and of a bad color; the average time of boiling for fresh meat is half an hour to every pound, salt meat requires half as long again, and smoked meat still longer; the lid of the saucepan should only be removed for skimming, which is an essential process.

E

Roasting chiefly depends on the skilful management of the fire, it is considered that a joint of eight pounds requires two hours roasting; when first put down it should be basted with fresh dripping, and afterwards with its own dripping, it should be sprinkled with salt, and repeatedly dredged with flour, which browns and makes it look rich and frothy.

Broiling requires a steady clear fire, free from flame and smoke, the gridiron should be· quite hot before the article is placed on it, and the bars should be rubbed with fat, or if the article is thin-skinned and delicate, with chalk; the gridiron should be held aslant to prevent the fat dripping into the fire; the bars of a gridiron should be close and fine. Frying is easier than broiling, the fat, oil or butter in which the article is fried must be boiling, but have ceased to bubble before it is put in the pan, or it will be greasy and black: there is now a new description of fryingpan, called a sauté pan, and which will be found extremely convenient for frying small cutlets or collops.

Stewing is a more elaborate mode of boiling; a gentle heat with frequent skimmings, are the points to be observed.

Glazing is done by brushing melted jelly over the article to be glazed and letting it cool, and then adding another coat, or in some cases two or three, this makes any cold meats or poultry have an elegant appearance.

Blanching makes the article plump and white. It should be set on the fire in cold water, boil up and then be immersed in cold water, where it should remain some little time. Larding (the French term is *Piqué*, which the inexperienced Jewish cook may not be acquainted with, we therefore use the term in common use) is a term given to a certain mode of garnishing the surface of meat or poultry : it is inserting small pieces of the fat of smoked meats, truffles, or tongue, which are trimmed into slips of equal length and size, into the flesh of the article at regular distances, and is effected by means of larding pins.

Poelée and Blanc, are terms used in modern cookery for a very expensive mode of stewing : it is done by stewing the article with meat, vegetables, and fat of smoked meats, all well seasoned ; instead of placing it to stew in water it is placed on slices of meat covered with slices of fat and the vegetables and seasoning added, then water enough to cover the whole is added.

Blanc differs from Poelée, in having a quantity of suet added, and being boiled down before the article is placed to stew in it.

Braising is a similar process to Poelée, but less meat and vegetable is used.

TO CLARIFY SUET.

Melt down with care fine fresh suet, either beef or veal, put it into a jar, and set it in a stew-pan of water to boil, putting in a sprig of rosemary, or a little orange flower water while melting, this is a very useful preparation and will be found, if adopted in English kitchens, to answer the purpose of lard and is far more delicate and wholesome : it should be well beaten till quite light with a wooden fork.

OLIO.

Put eight pounds of beef in sufficient water to cover it, when the water boils take out the meat, skim off the fat, and then return the meat to the stew-pan, adding at the same time two fine white cabbages without any of the stalk or hard parts; season with pepper, salt, and a tea-spoonful of white sugar, let it simmer on a slow fire for about five hours, about an hour before serving, add half a pound of *chorisa,* which greatly improves the flavor.

––––

AN EXCELLENT RECEIPT FOR STEWING A RUMP OF BEEF.

Chop fine a large onion, four bay leaves, and a little parsley, add to these half an ounce of ground ginger, a tea-spoonful of salt, a blade of mace, a little ground allspice, some lemon sliced, and some of the peel grated; rub all these ingredients well into the meat, then place it into a stew-pan with three parts of a cup of vinegar, a calf's-foot cut in small pieces and a pint of water, stew gently till tender, when the fat must be carefully skimmed off the gravy, which must be strained and poured over the meat.

––––

ALAMODE BEEF, OR SOUR MEAT.

Cover a piece of the ribs of beef boned and filletted, or a piece of the round with vinegar diluted with water, season with onions, pepper, salt, whole allspice, and three or four bay leaves, add a cup full of raspings, and let the whole stew gently for three or four hours, according to the weight of the meat; this dish is excellent when cold. A rump steak stewed in the same way will be found exceedingly fine.

———

K I M M E L   M E A T.

Place a small piece of the rump of beef, or the under cut of a sirloin in a deep pan with three pints of vinegar, two ounces of carraway seeds tied in a muslin bag, salt, pepper, and spices, cover it down tight, and bake thoroughly in a slow oven. This is a fine relish for luncheons.

———

BEEF AND BEANS.

Take a piece of brisket of beef, cover it with water, when boiling skim off the fat, add one quartern of French beans cut small, two onions cut in quarters, season with pepper and salt, and when nearly done take a dessert-spoonful of flour, one of coarse brown sugar, and a large tea-cup full of vinegar, mix them together and stir in with the beans, and continue stewing for about half an hour longer.

KUGEL AND COMMEAN.

Soak one pint of Spanish peas and one pint of Spanish beans all night in three pints of water; take two marrow bones, a calf's-foot, and three pounds of fine gravy-beef, crack the bones and tie them to prevent the marrow escaping, and put all together into a pan; then take one pound of flour, half a pound of shred suet, a little grated nutmeg and ground ginger, cloves and allspice, one pound of coarse brown sugar, and the crumb of a slice of bread, first soaked in water and pressed dry, mix all these ingredients together into a paste, grease a quart basin and put it in, covering the basin with a plate set in the middle of the pan with the beans, meat, &c. Cover the pan lightly down with coarse brown paper, and let it remain all the night and the next day, (until required) in a baker's oven, when done, take out the basin containing the pudding, and skim the fat from the gravy which must be served as soup; the meat, &c., is extremely savory and nutritious, but is not a very seemly dish for table. The pudding must be turned out of the basin, and a sweet sauce flavored with lemon and brandy is a fine addition.

SAUER KRAUT.

Boil about seven or eight pounds of beef, either brisket or a fillet off the shoulder, in enough water to cover it, when it has boiled for one hour, add as much sauer kraut, which is a German preparation, as may be approved, it should then stew gently for four hours and be served in a deep dish. The Germans are not very particular in removing the fat, but it is more delicate by so doing.

BEEF WITH CELERY,
AND WHITE BEANS AND PEAS.

Soak for twelve hours one pint of dried white peas, and half a pint of the same kind of beans, they must be well soaked, and if very dry, may require longer than twelve hours, put a nice piece of brisket of about eight pounds weight in a stew-pan with the peas and beans, and three heads of celery cut in small pieces, put water enough to cover, and season with pepper and salt only, let it all stew slowly till the meat is extremely tender and the peas and beans quite soft, then add four large lumps of sugar and nearly a tea-cup of vinegar; this is a very fine stew.

BEEF COLLOPS.

Cut thin slices off from any tender part,
divide them into pieces of the size of a wine
biscuit, flatten and flour them, and lightly fry
in clarified fat, lay them in a stew-pan with
good stock, season to taste, have pickled gherkins
chopped small, and add to the gravy a few minutes
before serving.

TO WARM COLD ROAST BEEF WHEN NOT SUFFI-CIENTLY DONE.

Cut it in slices, also slice some beetroot or
cucumber and put them in a saucepan with a
little gravy which need not be strong, two table-
spoonsful of vinegar, one of oil, pepper, salt, a
little chopped lettuce and a few peas, simmer till
the vegetables and meat are sufficiently dressed.

TO HASH BEEF.

The meat should be put on the fire in a little
broth or gravy, with a little fried onion, pepper,
salt, and a spoonful of ketchup, or any other
sauce at hand, let it simmer for about ten
minutes, then mix in a cup a little flour with a

little of the gravy, and pour it into the stewpan to thicken the rest; sippets of toast should be served with hashes, a little port wine, a pinch of saffron, or a piece *chorisa* may be considered great improvements.

STEAKS WITH CHESNUTS.

Take a fine thick steak, half fry it, then flour and place it in a stewpan with a little good beef gravy, season with cayenne pepper and salt, when it has simmered for about ten minutes, add a quarter of a hundred good chesnuts, peeled and the inner skin scraped off, let them stew with the steak till well done, this is a very nice dish, a little Espagnole sauce heightens the flavor.

A SIMPLE STEWED STEAK.

Put a fine steak in a stewpan with a large piece of clarified suet or fat, and a couple of onions sliced, let the steak fry for a few minutes, turning it several times; then cover the steak with gravy, or even water will answer the purpose, with a tea-cup full of button onions, or a

Spanish onion sliced, a little lemon peel, pepper, salt, and a little allspice; simmer till the steak is done, when the steak must be removed and the gravy be carefully skimmed, then add to it a little browning and a spoonful of mushroom ketchup; the steak must be kept on a hot stove or returned to the stewpan to warm up. If the gravy is not thick enough, stir in a little flour.

BRISKET STEWED WITH ONIONS AND RAISINS.

Stew about five pounds of brisket of beef in sufficient water to cover, season with allspice, pepper, salt, and nutmeg, and when nearly done, add four large onions cut in pieces and half a pound of raisins stoned, let them remain simmering till well done; and just before serving, stir in a tea-spoonful of brown sugar and a table spoonful of flour.

BRISKET STEWED.

Take about six or seven pounds of brisket of beef, place it in a stewpan with only enough water to cover it, season with a little spice tied in a bag; when the meat is tender and the spices sufficiently extracted to make the gravy rich and strong, part of it must be removed to another saucepan; have ready a variety of vegetables cut into small shapes, such as turnips, carrots, mushrooms, cauliflowers, or whatever may be in season; stew them gently till tender in the gravy, the meat must then be glazed and the gravy poured in the dish, and the vegetables arranged round.

BEEF RAGOUT.

Take a small well cut piece of lean beef, lard it with the fat of smoked beef, and stew it with good gravy, highly seasoned with allspice, cloves, pepper and salt; when the meat is well done remove it from the gravy, which skim carefully and free from every particle of fat, and add to it a glass of port wine, the juice of a lemon, half a tea-spoonful of cayenne pepper, and a little mushroom ketchup; the beef should be glazed when required to have an elegant appearance.

A few very small forcemeat balls must be poached in the gravy, which must be poured over the meat, and the balls arranged round the dish; this is a very savoury and pretty dish.

TO SALT BEEF.

This may be done by mixing a pound of common salt, half an ounce of saltpetre and one ounce of coarse brown sugar, and rubbing the meat well with it, daily for a fortnight or less, according to the weather, and the degree of salt that the meat is required to have. Or by boiling eight ounces of salt, eight ounces of sugar, and half an ounce of saltpetre in two quarts of water, and pouring it over the meat, and letting it stand in it for eight or ten days.

SPICED BEEF.

Take a fine thick piece of brisket of beef not fat, let it lay three days in a pickle, as above, take it out and rub in a mixture of spices consisting of equal quantities of ground all-spice, black pepper, cloves, ginger and nutmegs, and a little brown sugar, repeat this daily for a week, then cover it with pounded dried sweet herbs, roll or tie it tightly, put it into a pan with very little water, and bake slowly for eight hours, then take it out, untie it and put a heavy weight upon it; this it a fine relish when eaten cold.

SMOKED BEEF.

As there are seldom conveniences in private kitchens far smoking meats, it will generally be the best and cheapest plan to have them ready prepared for cooking. All kinds of meats smoked and salted, are to be met with in great perfection at all the Hebrew butchers.

Chorisa, that most refined and savoury of all sausages, is to be also procured at the same places. It is not only excellent fried in slices with poached eggs or stewed with rice, but imparts a delicious flavor to stews, soups, and sauces, and is one of the most useful resources of the Jewish kitchen.

A WHITE FRICANDEAU OF VEAL.

Take four or five pounds of breast of veal, or fillet from the shoulder; stuff it with a finely flavoured veal stuffing and put it into a stewpan with water sufficient to cover it, a calf's-foot cut in pieces is sometimes added, season with one onion, a blade of mace, white pepper and salt, and a sprig of parsley, stew the whole gently until the meat is quite tender, then skim and strain the gravy and stir in the beaten yolks of four eggs, and the juice of two lemons previously mixed smoothly with a portion of the gravy, button mushrooms, or pieces of celery stewed with the veal are sometimes added by way of varying the flavor, egg and forcemeat balls garnish the dish. When required to look elegant it should be piqué.

A BROWN FRICASSEE.

Cut a breast of veal in pieces, fry them lightly and put them into a stewpan with a good beef gravy, seasoned with white pepper, salt, a couple of sliced onions (previously browned in a little oil), and a piece of whole ginger, let it simmer very slowly for two hours taking care to remove the scum or fat, have ready some rich forcemeat and spread it about an inch thick over three cold hard boiled eggs, fry these for a few moments and put them in the saucepan with the veal; before serving, these balls should be cut in quarters, and the gravy rendered more savory by the addition of lemon juice and half a glass of white wine, or a table-spoonful of walnut liquor, if the gravy is not sufficiently thick by long stewing, a little browned flour may be stirred in.

CALF'S HEAD STEWED.

Clean and soak the head till the cheek-bone can be easily removed, then parboil it and cut it into pieces of moderate size, and place them in about a quart of stock made from shin of beef, the gravy must be seasoned highly with eschalots, a small head of celery, a small bunch of sweet herbs, an onion, a carrot, a little mace, a dozen cloves, a piece of lemon peel, and a sprig of parsley, salt and pepper; it must be strained before the head is added, fine forcemeat balls rolled in egg and fried are served in the dish, as well as small fritters made with the brains; when ready for serving, a glass and half of white wine and the juice of a lemon are added to the gravy.

CALVES-FEET WITH SPANISH SAUCE.

Having cleaned, boiled and split two fine feet, dip them into egg and bread crumbs mixed with chopped parsley and chalot, a few ground cloves, a little nutmeg, pepper and salt, fry them a fine brown, arrange them in the dish and pour the sauce over. Make the sauce in the following manner: slice two fine Spanish onions, put them in a saucepan, with some chopped truffles or mushrooms, a little suet, cayenne and white pepper, salt, one or two small lumps of white sugar, and let all simmer in some good strong stock till the gravy has nearly boiled away, then stir in a wine glass of Madeira wine, and a little lemon juice; it should then be returned to the saucepan, to be made thoroughly hot before serving.

CALF'S FEET AU FRITUR.

Simmer them for four hours in water till the meat can be taken easily from the bone, then cut them in handsome pieces, season with pepper and salt, dip them in egg, and sprinkle thickly with grated bread crumbs, and fry of a fine even brown; they may be served dry or with any sauce that may be approved.

The liquor should continue to stew with the bones, and can be used for jelly.

CALF'S FEET STEWED FOR INVALIDS.

Clean and soak a fine foot, put it on in very little water, let it simmer till tender, then cut it in pieces, without removing the bone, and

F

continue stewing for three hours, till they become perfectly soft; if the liquor boils away, add a little more water, but there should not be more liquor than can be served in the dish with the foot; the only seasoning requisite is a little salt and white pepper, and a sprig of parsley, or a pinch of saffron to improve the appearance; a little delicately-made thin egg sauce, with a flavor of lemon juice, may be served in a sauce-tureen if approved; sippets of toast or well boiled rice to garnish the dish, may also be added, and will not be an unacceptable addition.

TENDONS OF VEAL.

This is a very fine and nutritious dish; cut from the bones of a breast of veal the tendons which are round the front, trim and blanch them, put them with slices of smoked beef into a stewpan with some shavings of veal, a few herbs, a little sliced lemon, two or three onions, and a little broth; they must simmer for seven or eight hours; when done, thicken the gravy and add white wine and mushrooms and egg-balls; a few peas with the tendons will be found

excellent, a piece of mint and a little white
sugar will then be requisite.

FRICANDEAU OF VEAL.

Take a piece from the shoulder, about three
to four pounds, trim it and form it into a well
shaped even piece, the surface of which should
be quite smooth ; *piqué* it thickly, put it into a
stewpan with a couple of onions, a carrot sliced,
sweet herbs, two or three bay leaves, a large
piece of *chorissa* or a slice of the root of a
tongue smoked, a little whole pepper and salt ;
cover it with a gravy made from the trimmings
of the veal, and stew till extremely tender,
which can be proved by probing it with a fine
skewer, then reduce part of the gravy to a glaze,
glaze the meat with it and serve on a *pureé* of
vegetables.

COLLARED VEAL.

Remove the bones, gristle, &c., from a nice
piece of veal, the breast is the best part for the
purpose ; season the meat well with chopped
herbs, mace, pepper, and salt, then lay between
the veal slices of smoked tongue variegated

with beetroot, chopped parsley, and hard yolks of eggs, roll it up tightly in a cloth, simmer for some hours till tender; when done, it should have a weight laid on it to press out the liquor.

CURRIED VEAL.

Cut a breast of veal into pieces, fry lightly with a chopped onion, then rub the veal over with currie powder, put it into a good gravy of veal and beef, season simply with pepper, salt, and lemon juice.

Fowls curried are prepared in the same way.

CUTLETS.

Cut them into proper shape and beat them with a roller until the fibre of the meat is entirely broken; if this is not done, they will be hard; they must then be covered with egg and sprinkled with flour, or a preparation for cutlets may be spread over them, and then fry them of a fine brown, remove the cutlets to a hot dish, and add to the fat in which the cutlets have been fried, a spoonful of flour, a small cup of gravy, salt, pepper, and a little lemon juice or lemon pickle.

CUTLETS A LA FRANÇAISE.

French cooks cut them thinner than the English, and trim them into rounds of the size of a tea-cup; they must be brushed over with egg, and sprinkled with salt, white pepper, mushroom powder, and grated lemon peel; put them into a *sauté* pan and fry of a very light brown; pieces of bread, smoked meat or tongue cut of the same size as the cutlets, and prepared in the same manner, are laid alternately in the dish with them; they should be served without sauce and with a *purée* of mushrooms or spinach in the centre of the dish.

CUTLETS IN WHITE FRICASSEE.

Cut them in proper shapes, put them in a veal gravy made with the trimmings enough to cover them; season delicately, and let them simmer till quite tender, but not long enough to lose their shape; fresh button mushrooms and a piece of lemon peel are essential to this dish; when the meat is done remove it, take all fat from the gravy, and thicken it with the yolks of two beaten eggs; small balls of forcemeat in

which mushrooms must be minced should be
poached in the gravy when about to be served;
the meat must be returned to the saucepan to be
made hot, and when placed in the dish, garnish
with thin slices of lemon.

CUTLETS IN BROWN FRICASSEE.

They must be trimmed as above, fried slightly
and stewed in beef gravy, and seasoned according to the directions given for a brown fricassee
of veal; balis or fritters are always an improvement to the appearance of this dish.

BLANQUETTE OF VEAL.

Cut into thin pieces of the size of shillings and
half crowns, cold veal or poultry, lay it in a small
saucepan with a handful of fresh well cleaned
button mushrooms, pour over a little veal gravy,
only enough to cover them, with a piece of
clarified veal fat about the size of the yolk of a
hard boiled egg; flavor with a piece of lemon
peel, very little white pepper and salt, one small
lump of white sugar, and a little nutmeg, stew
all together for fifteen minutes, then pour over

a sauce prepared in a separate saucepan, made
with veal gravy, a little lemon juice, but not
much, and the beaten yolks of two eggs, let it
simmer for an instant and then serve it up in the
centre of a dish prepared with a wall of mashed
potatoes, delicately browned; a few truffles renders this dish more elegant.

MINCED VEAL.

Cut in small square pieces about the size of
dice, cold dressed veal, put it into a saucepan
with a little water or gravy, season simply with
salt, pepper, and grated or minced lemon peel,
the mince should be garnished with sippets of
toast.

MIROTON OF VEAL.

Mince finely some cold veal or poultry, add a
little grated tongue, or smoked beef, a few
crumbs of bread, sweet herbs, pepper, salt, parsley, and if approved, essence of lemon, mix all
well with two or three eggs, and a very small
quantity of good gravy; grease a mould, put in

the above ingredients and bake for three-quarters
of an hour; turn out with care, and serve with
mushroom sauce.

————

FRICONDELLES.

Prepare cold veal or poultry as in the last
receipt, add instead of crumbs of bread, a French
roll soaked in white gravy, mix with it the same
ingredients, and form it into two shapes to imi-
tate small chickens or sweetbreads; sprinkle with
crumbs of bread, and place in a frying-pan as
deep as a shallow saucepan; when they have
fried enough to become set, pour enough weak
gravy in the pan to cover the fricondelles, and
let them stew in it gently, place them both in
the same dish, and pour over any well thickened
sauce that may be selected.

————

ANOTHER SORT.

Prepare four small pieces of veal to serve in
one dish, according to the directions given for
fricandeau of veal; these form a very pretty
entrée; the pieces of veal should be about the
size of pigeons.

SMOKED VEAL.

Take a fine fat thick breast of veal, bone it, lay it in pickle, according to the receipt to salt meat, hang it for three or four weeks in wood-smoke, and it will prove a very fine savoury relish, either boiled and eaten cold, or fried as required.

SWEETBREADS ROASTED.

First soak them in warm water, and then blanch them; in whatever manner they are to be dressed, this is essential; they may be prepared in a variety of ways, the simplest is to roast them; for this they have only to be covered with egg and bread crumbs, seasoned with salt and pepper, and finished in a Dutch oven or cradle spit, frequently basting with clarified veal suet; they may be served either dry with a *purée* of vegetables, or with a brown gravy.

SWEETBREADS STEWED WHITE.

After soaking and blanching, stew them in veal gravy, and season with celery, pepper, salt, nutmeg, a little mace, and a piece of lemon peel, they should be served with a fine white sauce, the gravy in which they are stewed will form the basis for it, with the addition of yolks of eggs and mushroom essence; French cooks would adopt the *velouté* or *bechamél* sauce; Jerusalem artichokes cut the size of button mushrooms, are a suitable accompaniment as a garnish.

SWEETBREADS STEWED BROWN.

After soaking and blanching, fry them till brown, then simmer gently in beef gravy seasoned highly with smoked meat, nutmeg, pepper, salt, a small onion stuck with cloves, and a very little whole allspice; the gravy must be slightly thickened, and morels and truffles are generally added; small balls of delicate forcemeat are also an improvement. The above receipts are adapted for sweetbreads fricasseed, except that they must be cut in pieces for fricassees, and pieces of meat or poultry are added to them; sweetbreads when dressed whole look better *piqués*.

A DELICATE RECEIPT FOR ROAST MUTTON.

Put the joint in a saucepan, cover it with cold water, let it boil for half an hour, have the spit and fire quite ready, and remove the meat from the saucepan, and place it immediately down to roast, baste it well, dredge it repeatedly with flour, and sprinkle with salt; this mode of roasting mutton removes the strong flavor that is so disagreeable to some tastes.

MUTTON STEWED WITH CELERY.

Take the best end of a neck of mutton, or a fillet taken from the leg or shoulder, place it in a stewpan with just enough water to cover it, throw in a carrot and turnip, and season, but not too highly; when nearly done remove the meat and strain off the gravy, then return both to the stewpan with forcemeat balls and some fine celery cut in small pieces; let all stew gently till perfectly done, then stir in the yolks of two eggs, a little flour, and the juice of half a lemon, which must be mixed with a little of the gravy before pouring in the stewpan, and care must be taken to prevent curdling.

A SIMPLE WAY OF DRESSING MUTTON.

Take the fillet off a small leg or shoulder of
mutton, rub it well over with egg and seasoning,
and partly roast it, then place it in a stewpan
with a little strong gravy, and stew gently till
thoroughly done; this dish is simple, but exceedingly nice; a few balls or fritters to garnish
will improve it.

MAINTENON CUTLETS.

This is merely broiling or frying cutlets in a
greased paper, after having spread on them a
seasoning prepared as follows: make a paste of
bread crumbs, chopped parsley, nutmeg, pepper,
salt, grated lemon peel, and thyme, with a couple
of beaten eggs; a piquante sauce should be
served in a tureen.

A HARRICOT.

Cut off the best end of a neck of mutton into
chops, flour and partly fry them, then lay them
in a stewpan with carrots, sliced turnips cut in
small round balls, some button onions, and cover
with water; skim frequently, season with pepper

and salt to taste, color the gravy with a little browning and a spoonful of mushroom powder.

IRISH STEW.

Is the same as above, excepting that the meat is not previously fried, and that potatoes are used instead of turnips and carrots.

MUTTON A L'HISPANIOLA.

Take a small piece of mutton, either part of a shoulder or a fillet of the leg, partly roast it, then put it in a stewpan with beef gravy enough to cover it, previously seasoned with herbs, a carrot and turnip; cut in quarters three large Spanish onions, and place in the stewpan round the meat; a stuffing will improve it, and care must be taken to free the gravy from every particle of fat.

MUTTON COLLOPS.

Take from a fine knuckle a couple of slices, cut and trim them in collops the size of a tea cup, flatten them and spread over each side a forcemeat for cutlets, and fry them; potatoe or

Jerusalem artichokes cut in slices of the same size and thickness, or pieces of bread cut with a fluted cutter, prepared as the collops and fried, must be placed alternately in the dish with them ; they may be served with a pure simple gravy, or very hot and dry on a napkin, garnished with fried parsley and slices of lemon.

The knuckle may be used in the following manner : put it on with sufficient water to cover it, season it and simmer till thoroughly done, thicken the gravy with prepared barley, and flavor it with lemon pickle, or capers ; it should be slightly colored with saffron, and celery sauce may be served as an accompaniment, or the mutton may be served on a fine *purée* of turnips.

MUTTON CUTLETS.

Have a neck of mutton, cut the bones short, and remove the chine bone completely; cut chops off so thin that every other one shall be without bone, trim them carefully, that all the chops shall bear the same appearance, then flatten them well; cover them with a cutlet preparation, and fry of a delicate brown; a fine *purée* of any vegetable that may be approved,

or any sauce that may be selected, should be
served with them; they may be arranged in
various ways in the dish, either round the dish
or in a circle in the centre, so that the small
part of the cutlets shall almost meet; if the
latter, the *purée* should garnish round them
instead of being in the centre of the dish.

MUTTON HAM.

Choose a fine leg of mutton, rub it in daily
with a mixture of three ounces of brown sugar,
two ounces of common salt, and half an ounce
of saltpetre, continue this process for a fortnight,
then hang it to dry in wood smoke for ten days
longer.

LAMB AND SPREW.

Take a fine neck or breast of lamb, put it in
stewpan with as much water as will cover it, add
to it a bundle of sprew cut in pieces of two inches
in length, a small head of celery cut small, and
one onion, pepper, salt, and a sprig of parsley,
let it simmer gently till the meat and sprew are
tender; a couple of lumps of sugar improves the
flavor; there should not be too much liquor, and

all fat must be removed; the sprew should surround the meat when served, and also be thickly laid over it.

LAMB AND PEAS.

Take the best end of a neck of lamb, either keep it whole or divide it into chops as may be preferred, put it into a saucepan with a little chopped onion, pepper, salt, and a small quantity of water; when half done add half a peck of peas, half a lettuce cut fine, a little mint, and a few lumps of sugar, and let it stew thoroughly; when done, there must not be too much liquor; cutlets of veal or beef are also excellent dressed as above. Although this is a spring dish it may be almost equally well dressed in winter, by substituting small mutton cutlets and preserved peas, which may be met with at any of the best Italian warehouses; a breast or neck of lamb may also be stewed whole in the same manner.

LAMB CUTLETS WITH CUCUMBERS.

Take two fine cucumbers, peel and cut them lengthways, lay them in vinegar for an hour, then stew them in good stock till tender, when

stir in the yolks of two or three eggs, a little
flour and essence of lemon, which must all be
first mixed up together with a little of the stock,
have ready some cutlets trimmed and fried a
light brown, arrange them round the dish and
pour the cucumbers in the centre.

A NICE RECEIPT FOR SHOULDER OF LAMB.

Half boil it, score it and squeeze over lemon
juice, and cover with grated bread crumbs, egg
and parsley, broil it over a clear fire and put it to
brown in a Dutch oven, or grill and serve with a
sauce seasoned with lemon pickle and chopped
mint.

A CASSEREET, AN EAST INDIA DISH.

Take two pounds of lamb chops, or mutton
may be substituted, place them in a stewpan,
cover with water or gravy, season only with pepper and salt, when the chops are half done,
carefully skim off the fat and add two table
spoonsful of cassereet, stir it in the gravy which
should not be thickened, and finish stewing
gently till done enough; rice should accompany
this dish.

G

TURKEY BONED AND FORCED.

A turkey thus prepared may be either boiled or roasted; there are directions for boning poultry which might be given, but it is always better to let the poulterer do it; when boned it must be filled with a fine forcemeat, which may be varied in several ways, the basis should be according to the receipt given for veal stuffings, forcemeats, sausage meat, tongue, and mushrooms added as approved. When boiled it is served with any fine white sauce, French cooks use the velouté or béchamel. When roasted, a cradle spit is very convenient, but if there is not one the turkey must be carefully tied to the spit.

FOWLS BONED AND FORCED.

The above directions serve also for fowls.

A SAVOURY WAY OF ROASTING A FOWL.

Fill it with a fine seasoning, and just before it is ready for serving, baste it well with clarified veal suet, and sprinkle it thickly with very dry crumbs of bread, repeat this two or three times; then place it in the dish, and serve with a fine

brown gravy well flavored with lemon juice;
delicate forcemeat fritters should be also served
in the dish.

BOILED FOWLS.

Are served with a fine white sauce, and are
often garnished with pieces of white cauliflower,
or vegetable marrow, the chief object is to keep
them white; it is best to select white legged
poultry for boiling, as they prove whiter when
dressed.

AMNASTICH.

Stew gently one pint of rice in one quart of
strong gravy till it begins to swell, then add an
onion stuck with cloves, a bunch of sweet herbs,
and a chicken stuffed with forcemeat, let it stew
with the rice till thoroughly done, then take it
up and stir in the rice, the yolks of four eggs,
and the juice of a lemon; serve the fowl in the
same dish with the rice, which should be colored
to a fine yellow with saffron.

FOWLS STEWED WITH RICE AND CHORISA.

Boil a fowl in sufficient water or gravy to

cover it, when boiling for ten minutes, skim off
the fat and add half a pound of rice, and one
pound of *chorisa* cut in about four pieces, season
with a little white pepper, salt, and a pinch of
saffron to color it, and then stew till the rice is
thoroughly tender; there should be no gravy
when served, but the rice ought to be perfectly
moist.

CURRIED CHICKEN.

See curried veal. Undressed chicken is considered best for a curry, it must be cut in small
joints, the directions for curried veal are equally
adapted for fowls.

A NICE METHOD OF DRESSING FOWL
AND SWEETBREAD.

Take a fowl and blanch it, also a fine sweet
bread, parboil them, then cut off in smooth well
shaped slices, all the white part of the fowl, and
slice the sweetbread in similar pieces, place
them together in a fine well-flavoured veal
gravy; when done, serve neatly in the dish, and
pour over a fine white sauce, any that may be
approved, the remainder of the fowl must be
cut up in small joints or pieces, not separated

from the bone, and fried to become brown, then place them in a stew-pan with forcemeat balls, truffles, and morels; pour over half or three quarters of a pint of beef gravy, and simmer till finished; a little mushroom ketchup, or lemon-pickle may be added; in this manner two very nice *entrées* may be formed.

BLANKETTE OF FOWL.

See blankette of veal.

TO STEW DUCK WITH GREEN PEAS.

Stuff and half roast a duck, then put it into a stew-pan with an onion sliced, a little mint and about one pint of beef gravy, add after it has simmered half an hour, a quart of green peas, and simmer another half hour; a little lump sugar is requisite.

TO WARM COLD POULTRY.

Cut up the pieces required to be dressed, spread over them a seasoning as for cutlets, and fry them; pour over a little good gravy, and garnish with sippets of toast and sliced lemon, or place them in an edging of rice or mashed potatoes.

BROILED FOWL AND MUSHROOMS.

Truss a fine fowl as if for boiling, split it down the back, and broil gently; when nearly done, put it in a stewpan with a good gravy, add a pint of fresh button mushrooms, season to taste; a little mushroom powder and lemon juice improve the flavour.

PIGEONS.

To have a good appearance they should be larded and stuffed; glazing is also an improvement, they form a nice *entrée*; they may be stewed in a strong gravy; when done enough, remove the pigeons, thicken the gravy, add a few forcemeat and egg balls, and serve in the dish with the pigeons. Or they may be split down the back, broiled, and then finished in the stew-pan.

STEWED GIBLETS.

Scald one or more sets of giblets, set them on the fire with a little veal or chicken, or both, in a good gravy; season to taste, thicken the gravy, and color it with browning, flavor with mushroom powder and lemon-juice and one glass

of white wine; forcemeat balls should be added
a few minutes before serving, and garnish with
thin slices of hard boiled eggs.

DUTCH TOAST.

Take the remains of any cold poultry or meat,
mince it and season highly; add to it any cold
dressed vegetable, mix it up with one or more
eggs, and let it simmer till hot in a little gravy;
have ready a square of toast, and serve it on it;
squeeze over a little lemon-juice, and sprinkle
with white pepper. Vegetables prepared in this
way are excellent; cauliflower simmered in
chicken broth, seasoned delicately and minced
on toast, is a nutritive good luncheon for an
invalid.

TIMBALE DE MACCARONI.

This is a very pretty dish. The maccaroni
must be boiled in water till it slightly swells, and
is soft enough to cut; it must be cut into short
pieces about two inches in length. Grease a
mould, and stick the maccaroni closely together
all over the mould; when this is done, and which
will require some patience, fill up the space with

friccassee of chicken, sweetbreads, or whatever
may be liked; close the mould carefully, and
boil. Rich white sauce is usually served with
it, but not poured over the timbale, as it would
spoil the effect of the honeycomb appearance,
which is very pretty.

A SAVOURY PIE FOR PERSONS OF DELICATE DIGESTION.

Cut up fowl and sweetbread, lay in the dish
in alternate layers with meat, jelly, and the
yolks of hard-boiled eggs without the whites, and
flavor with lemon-juice, white pepper, and salt;
cover with rice prepared as follows: boil half a
pound of rice in sufficient water to permit it to
swell; when tender beat it up to a thick paste
with the yolk of one or two eggs, season with a
little salt, and spread it over the dish thickly.
The fowl and sweetbread should have been previously simmered till half done in a little weak
broth; the pie must be baked in a gentle oven,
and if the rice will not brown sufficiently, finish
with a salamander.

DESCAIDES.

Take the livers of chickens or any other poultry; stew it gently in a little good gravy seasoned with a little onion, mushroom essence,
pepper, and salt; when tender, remove the livers,
place them on a paste board, and mince them;
return them to the saucepan, and stir in the
yolks of one or two eggs, according to the quantity of liver, until the gravy becomes thick;
have a round of toast ready on a hot plate, and
serve it on the toast; this is a very nice luncheon
or supper dish.

CHAPTER V.

Vegetables and Sundries.

––––

DIRECTIONS FOR CLEANING AND BOILING VEGETABLES.

VEGETABLES are extremely nutritious when sufficiently boiled, but are unwholesome and indigestible when not thoroughly dressed; still they should not be over boiled, or they will lose their flavor.

Vegetables should be shaken to get out any insects, and laid in water with a little salt.

Soft water is best suited for boiling vegetables, and they require plenty of water; a little salt should be put in the saucepan with them, and the water should almost invariably be boiling when they are put in.

Potatoes are much better when steamed. Peas

and several other vegetables are also improved by this mode of cooking them, although it is seldom adopted in England.

MASHED POTATOES.

Boil till perfectly tender; let them be quite dry, and press them through a cullender, or mash and beat them well with a fork; add a piece of butter, and milk, or cream, and continue beating till they are perfectly smooth; return them to the saucepan to warm, or they may be browned before the fire. The chief art is to beat them sufficiently long, which renders them light.

Potatoe balls are mashed potatoes formed into balls glazed with the yolk of egg, and browned with a salamander.

POTATO WALL, OR EDGING.

Raise a wall of finely-mashed potatoes, of two or three inches high, round the dish; form it with a spoon to the shape required, brush it over with egg, and put it in the oven to become hot and brown; if it does not brown nicely, use the salamander. Rice is arranged the same way to

edge curries or fricassees ; it must be first boiled
till tender.

POTATOE SHAVINGS.

Take four fine large potatoes, and having
peeled them, continue to cut them up as if peel-
ing them in ribbons of equal width ; then throw
the shavings into a frying-pan, and fry of a fine
brown ; they must be constantly moved with a
silver fork to keep the pieces separate. They
should be laid on a cloth to drain, and placed
in the dish lightly.

THE FRENCH WAY OF DRESSING SPINACH.

Wash and boil till tender, then squeeze and
strain it ; press it in a towel till almost dry ; put
it on a board, and chop it as finely as possible ;
then return it to the saucepan, with butter, pepper, and salt ; stir it all the time, and let it boil
fast.

STEWED SPINACH.

Scald and chop some spinach small ; cut up
an onion ; add pepper and salt and brown sugar,

with a little vinegar, stew all together gently; serve with poached eggs or small forcemeat fritters. This forms a pretty side-dish, and is also a nice way of dressing spinach to serve in the same dish with cutlets.

TO STEW SPANISH BEANS AND PEAS.

Soak the beans over night in cold water; they must be stewed in only sufficient water to cover them, with two table spoonsful of oil, a little pepper and salt, and white sugar. When done they should be perfectly soft and tender.

PEAS STEWED WITH OIL.

Put half a peck of peas into a stew-pan, half a lettuce chopped small, a little mint, a small onion cut up, two table-spoonsful of oil, and a dessert-spoonful of powdered sugar, with water sufficient to cover the peas, watching, from time to time, that they do not become too dry; let them stew gently, taking care that they do not burn, till perfectly soft. When done they should look of a yellowish brown.

French beans, brocoli, and greens, stewed in the above manner will be found excellent.

CUCUMBER MANGO.

Cut a large cucumber in half, length ways, scoop out the seedy part, and lay it in vinegar that has been boiled with mustard-seed, a little garlic, and spices, for twenty-four hours, then fill the cucumber with highly-seasoned force-meat, and stew it in a rich gravy, the cucumber must be tied to keep it together.

CABBAGE AND RICE.

Scald till tender a fine summer white cabbage, then chop it up small, and put it into a stew-pan, with a large cup of rice, also previously scalded, add a little water, a large piece of butter, salt and pepper; let it stew gently till thoroughly done, stirring from time to time, and adding water and butter to prevent its getting too thick; there should be no gravy in the dish when served.

PALESTINE SALAD.

Take a dozen fine Jerusalem artichokes, boil till tender, let the water strain off, and when cold cut them in quarters, and pour over a fine salad mixture; the artichokes should lay in the sauce half an hour before serving. This salad is a very refreshing one, and has the advantage of being extremely wholesome.

A SPRING DISH.

Take one quart of young peas, a little mint, a few lumps of sugar, a little salt and white pepper, simmer them gently in one pint of water, when the peas are half done, throw in small dumplings made of paste, as if for short crust, and sweetened with a little brown sugar, beat up two eggs, and drop in a spoonful at a time, just before serving; it will require a deep dish, as the liquor is not to be strained off. Some prefer the eggs poached.

CARROTS AU BEURRE.

Boil them enough to be perfectly tender, then cut them in quarters, and again in lengths of three inches, drain them from the water, and put to them a piece of butter, salt and pepper, and simmer them for a few minutes without boiling; a large piece of butter must be used.

French beans are good dressed in the same
way.

PUREE OF VEGETABLES.

Take any vegetable that may be approved,
boil till well done, drain away all water, reduce
the vegetable to a pulp, and add to it any fine
sauce, to make it of the consistency of a very
thick custard.

JERUSALEM ARTICHOKES FRIED.

Cut in slices after parboiling them, dip in
batter, and fry.

STEWED RED CABBAGE.

Clean and remove the outer leaves, slice it as
thinly as possible, put it in a saucepan with a
large piece of butter, and a tea cup full of water,
salt and pepper; let it stew slowly till very
tender.

MUSHROOMS AU NATUREL.

Clean some fine fresh mushrooms, put them
in a saucepan with a large piece of butter,

pepper and salt; let them simmer until tender, and serve them with no other sauce than that in which they have been dressed. Also stewed in a veal gravy, and served with white sauce on a toast, they form a nice and pretty dish.

The large flap mushrooms may be stewed in gravy, or simply broiled, seasoned with cayenne pepper, salt, and lemon juice.

DRY TOMATO SOUP.

Brown a couple of onions in a little oil, about two table-spoonsful or more, according to the number of tomatos; when hot, add about six tomatos cut and peeled, season with cayenne pepper and salt, and let the whole simmer for a short time, then cut thin slices of bread, and put as much with the tomatos as will bring them to the consistency of a pudding; it must be well beaten up, stir in the yolks of two or three eggs, and two ounces of butter warmed; turn the whole into a deep dish and bake it very brown. Crumbs of bread should be strewed over the top, and a little warmed butter poured over.

H

DEVILLED BISCUITS.

Butter some biscuits on both sides, and pepper
them well, make a paste of either chopped anchovies, or fine cheese, and spread it on the
biscuit, with mustard and cayenne pepper, and
grill them.

——

SAVOURY EGGS.

Boil some eggs hard, put them into cold water,
cut them into halves, take out the yolks, beat
them up in a mortar with grated hung beef, fill
the halves with this mixture, fry lightly, and
serve with brown gravy

——

SAVOURY CHEESE CAKES.

Grate finely an equal quantity of stale bread
and good cheese, season with a little pepper and
salt, mix into a batter with eggs, form into thin
cakes and fry.

——

SCALLOPED EGGS.

Poach lightly three or four eggs, place them
in a dish, pour upon them a little warm butter;

sprinkle with pepper, salt, and nutmeg, strew over with crumbs of bread, and brown before the fire.

MACCARONI AND CHEESE.

Boil some maccaroni in milk or water until tender, then drain them and place on a dish with bits of butter and grated Parmesan cheese; when the dish is filled grate more cheese over it and brown before the fire.

A FINE RECEIPT FOR A SAVOURY OMELETTE.

Break four eggs, beat them up till thin enough to pass through a hair sieve, then beat them up till perfectly smooth and thin; a small omelette frying-pan is necessary for cooking it well. Dissolve in it a piece of butter, about an ounce and a half, pour in the egg, and as soon as it rises and is firm, slide it on to a warm plate and fold it over; it should only be fried on one side, and finely minced herbs should be sprinkled over the unfried side with pepper and salt. A salamander is frequently held over the unfried side of the omelette to take off the rawness it may otherwise have.

CHORISA OMELETTE.

Add to the eggs, after they are well beaten as
directed in the last receipt, half a tea-cup full of
finely minced *chorisa;* this omelette must be
lightly fried on both sides, or the salamander
held over long enough to dress the *chorisa.*

RAMAKINS.

Mix together three eggs, one ounce of warmed
butter, and two of fine cheese grated, and bake
in small patty pans.

RISSOLES.

Make a fine forcemeat of any cold meat, poultry, or fish, enclose it in a very rich puff paste,
rolled out extremely thin.   They may be made
into balls or small triangular turnovers, or into
long narrow ribbons; the edges must be pressed
together, that they may not burst in frying.
They form a pretty dish.

CROQUETTES.

Pound any cold poultry, meat, or fish, make
it into a delicate forcemeat ; the flavor can be

varied according to taste; minced mushrooms, herbs, parsley, grated lemon peel, are suitable for poultry and veal; minced anchovies should be used instead of mushrooms when the croquettes are made of fish. Form the mixture into balls or oval shapes the size of small eggs; dip them into beaten eggs, thickly sprinkle with bread crumbs or pounded vermicelli, and fry of a handsome brown.

CASSEROLE AU RIZ.

Boil some rice till quite tender, make it into a firm paste with one egg and a couple of tablespoons of strong gravy; then line the inside of a mould with the paste of sufficient thickness to turn out without breaking. Some cooks fill the mould instead of lining it only, and scoop away the centre. After it is turned out the rice must stand till cold, before it is removed from the mould; then fill the rice with friccassee of fowl and sweetbread, with a rich white sauce, and place it in the oven to become hot and brown. The mould used for a casserole is oval and fluted, and resembles a cake mould. It is as well to observe, it cannot be made in a jelly mould.

A FONDU.

Make into a batter one ounce and a half of potatoe flour, with the same quantity of grated cheese and of butter, and a quarter of a pint of milk or cream; add a little salt, very little pepper, and the well-beaten yolks of four fine fresh eggs; when all this is well mixed together, pour in the whites of the eggs, well whisked to a froth; pour the mixture into a deep soup plate or dish, used expressly for the purpose, and bake in a moderate oven. The dish should be only half filled with the *fondu*, as it will rise very high. It must be served the moment it is ready, or it will fall. It is a good plan to hold a salamander over it while being brought to table.

PETITS FONDEAUS.

Make a batter as for a fondu, but use rice flour or arrow root instead of potatoe flour; add the egg in the same manner as for a fondu, and pour the mixture into small paper trays fringed round the top. The mixture should only half fill the trays or cases.

CHAPTER VI.

Pastry.

DIRECTIONS FOR MAKING PASTE.

To make good light paste requires much practice; as it is not only from the proportions, but from the manner of mixing the various ingredients, that paste acquires its good or bad qualities.

Paste should be worked up very lightly, and no strength or pressure used; it should be rolled out *from you*, as lightly as possible. A marble slab is better than a board to make paste on.

The flour should be dried for some time before the fire previously to being used. In forming it into paste it should be wetted as little as possible, to prevent its being tough. It is a great mistake to imagine *lard* is better adapted for pastry than butter or clarified fat; it may make the paste lighter, but neither the color nor the flavor will be nearly so good, and the saving is extremely trifling.

To ensure lightness, paste should be set in the oven directly it is made.

Puff paste requires a brisk oven.

Butter should be added to the paste in small pieces.

The more times the paste is folded and rolled, if done with a light hand and the butter added with skill, the richer and lighter it will prove. It is no longer customary to line the dish for pies and fruit tarts.

PLAIN PUFF PASTE.

Mix a pound of flour into a stiff paste with a little water, first having rubbed into it about two ounces of butter, then roll it out; add by degrees the remainder of the butter (there should be altogether half a pound of butter), fold the paste and roll about two or three times.

VERY RICH PUFF PASTE.

Mix in the same manner equal quantities of butter and flour, taking care to have the flour dried for a short time before the fire ; it may be folded and rolled five or six times. This paste is well suited to vol-au-vents and tartlets ; an egg well beaten and mixed with the paste is sometimes added.

PLAIN SHORT CRUST.

Put half a pound of fresh butter to a pound of flour, add the yolks of two eggs and a little powdered sugar, mix into a paste with water, and roll out once.

EGG PASTE, CALLED IN MODERN COOKERY NOUILLES.

This is formed by making a paste of flour and beaten eggs, without either butter or water ; it must be rolled out extremely thin and left to dry ; it may then be cut into narrow strips or stamped with paste cutters. It is more fashionable in soups than vermicelli.

BEEF DRIPPING PASTE.

Mix half a pound of clarified dripping into one pound of flour; work it into a paste with water, and roll out twice. This is a good paste for a common meat pie.

GLAZE FOR PASTRY.

When the pastry is nearly baked, brush it over with white of egg, cover it thickly with sifted sugar, and brown it in the oven, or it may be browned with a salamander.

For savory pies beat the yolk of an egg, dip a paste-brush into it, and lay it on the crust before baking.

FRUIT TARTS OR PIES.

A fruit tart is so common a sweet that it is scarcely necessary to give any directions concerning it. Acid fruits are best stewed before putting into a pie: the usual proportions are half a pound of sugar to a quart of fruit—not quite so much if the fruit is ripe; the fruit should be laid high in the middle of the dish, to make the pie a good shape. It is the fashion to lay over the crust, when nearly baked, an icing of the whites of eggs whisked with sugar; the tart or pie is then replaced in the oven.

A VERY FINE SAVOURY PIE.

Lay a fine veal cutlet, cut in pieces and seasoned, at the bottom of the dish; lay over it a layer of smoked beef fat, then a layer of fine cold jelly made from gravy-beef and veal, then hard boiled eggs in slices, then chicken or sweetbread, and then again the jelly, and so on till the dish is filled; put no water, and season highly with lemon-juice, essence of mushroom, pepper, salt, and nutmeg; also, if approved, a blade of mace: small cakes of fine forcemeat are an improvement; cover with a fine puff paste, and brush over with egg, and bake.

TARTLETS.

Make a very rich light puff paste, and roll it out to half an inch of thickness; it should be cut with fluted paste-cutters, lightly baked, and the centre scooped out afterwards, and the sweet-

meat or jam inserted ; a pretty dish of pastry
may be made by cutting the paste in ribbons of
three inches in length, and one and a half in
width; bake them lightly, and pile them one
upon another, with jam between each, in the
form of a cone.

CHEESECAKES.

Warm four ounces of butter, mix it with the same
quantity of loaf-sugar sifted, grate in the rind of
three lemons, squeeze in the juice of one, add
three well-beaten eggs, a little nutmeg, and a
spoonful of brandy; put this mixture into small
tins lined with a light puff paste, and bake.

Cheesecakes can be varied by putting almonds
beaten instead of the lemon, or by substituting
Seville oranges, and adding a few slices of candied orange and lemon peel.

GIBLET PIE.

Prepare the giblets as for *"stewed giblets,"*
they should then be laid in a deep dish, covered
with a puff paste, and baked.

MOLINA PIE.

Mince finely cold veal or chicken, with smoked beef or tongue; season well, add lemon-juice and a little nutmeg, let it simmer in a small quantity of good beef or veal gravy; while on the fire, stir in the yolks of four eggs, put it in a dish to cool, and then cover with a rich pastry, and bake it.

VOL AU VENT.

This requires the greatest lightness in the pastry, as all depends upon its rising when baked; it should be rolled out about an inch and a half in thickness, cut it with a fluted tin of the size of the dish in which it is to be served. Also cut a smaller piece, which must be rolled out considerably thinner than an inch, to serve as a lid for the other part; bake both pieces, and when done, scoop out the crumb of the largest, and fill it with a white fricassee of chicken, sweetbread, or whatever may be selected; the sauce should be well thickened, or it would soften, and run through the crust.

A VOL-AU-VENT OF FRUIT.

It is now the fashion to fill *vol-au-vents* with fruits richly stewed with sugar until the syrup is almost a jelly; it forms a very pretty entremêt.

PETITS VOL-AU-VENTS.

These are made in the same way, but cut in small rounds, the crumb of the larger is scooped out, and the hollow filled with any of the varieties of patty preparations or preserved fruits.

MINCE PIES.

Grease and line tin patty-pans with a fine puff paste rolled out thin; fill them with mincemeat, cover them with another piece of paste, moisten the edges, close them carefully, cut them evenly round, and bake them about half an hour in a well-heated oven.

PATTY MEATS

May be prepared from any dressed materials, such as cold dressed veal, beef and mutton,

poultry, sweetbreads, and fish; the chief art
is to mince them properly, and give them
the appropriate flavor and sauce; for veal,
sweetbreads, and poultry, which may be used
together or separately, the usual seasonings are
mace, nutmeg, white pepper, salt, mushrooms
minced, or in powder, lemon-peel, and sometimes the juice also; the mince is warmed in a
small quantity of white sauce, not too thin, and
the patty crusts, when ready baked, are filled
with it.

For beef and mutton the seasonings are salt,
pepper, allspice, a few sweet herbs powdered, with
the addition, if approved, of a little ketchup;
the mince must be warmed in strong well-
thickened beef gravy.

If the mince is of fish, season with anchovy
sauce, nutmeg, lemon-peel, pepper and salt;
warm it in a sauce prepared with butter, flour,
and milk or cream, worked together smoothly
and stirred till it thickens; the mince is then
simmered in it for a few minutes, till hot; the
seasonings may be put with the sauces, instead
of with the mince.

CHAPTER VII.

——

Sweet Dishes, Puddings, Cakes, &c.

GENERAL REMARKS.

THE freshness of all ingredients for puddings is of great importance.

Dried fruits should be carefully picked, and sometimes washed and should then be dried. Rice, sago, and all kinds of seed should be soaked and well washed before they are mixed into puddings.

Half an hour should be allowed for boiling a bread pudding in a half pint basin, and so on in proportion.

All puddings of the custard kind require gentle boiling, and when baked must be set in a moderate oven.

By whisking to a solid froth the whites of the eggs used for any pudding, and stirring them into it at the moment of placing it in the oven, it will become exceedingly light and rise high in the dish.

All baked puddings should be baked in tin moulds in the form of a deep pie dish, but slightly fluted, it should be well greased by pouring into it a little warmed butter, and then turned upside down for a second, to drain away the superfluous butter; then sprinkle, equally all over, sifted white sugar, or dried crumbs of bread, then pour the pudding mixture into the mould; it should, when served, be turned out of the mould, when it will look rich and brown, and have the appearance of a cake.

To ensure the lightness of cakes, it is necessary to have all the ingredients placed for an hour or more before the fire, that they may all be warm and of equal temperature; without this precaution, cakes will be heavy even when the best ingredients are employed. Great care and experience are required in the management of the oven; to ascertain when a cake is sufficiently baked, plunge a knife into it, draw it instantly away, when, if the blade is sticky, return the

I

cake to the oven ; if, on the contrary, it appears unsoiled the cake is ready.

The lightness of cakes depends upon the ingredients being beaten well together. All stiff cakes may be beaten with the hand, but pound cakes, sponge, &c., should be beaten with a whisk or spoon.

BOLA D'AMOR.

The recipe for this much celebrated and exquisite confection is simpler than may be supposed from its elaborate appearance, it requires chiefly care, precision, and attention. Clarify two pounds of white sugar ; to ascertain when it is of a proper consistency, drop a spoonful in cold water, form it into a ball, and try if it sounds when struck against a glass; when it is thus tested, take the yolks of twenty eggs, mix them up gently and pass them through a sieve, then have ready a funnel, the hole of which must be about the size of vermicelli ; hold the funnel over the sugar, while it is boiling over a charcoal fire ; pour the eggs through, stirring the sugar all the time, and taking care to hold the funnel at such a distance from the sugar, as to admit of

the egg dropping into it. When the egg has
been a few minutes in the sugar, it will be hard
enough to take out with a silver fork, and must
then be placed on a drainer; continue adding
egg to the boiling sugar till enough is obtained;
there should be previously prepared one pound
of sweet almonds, finely pounded and boiled in
sugar, clarified with orange flower-water only;
place in a dish a layer of this paste, over which
spread a layer of citron cut in thin slices, and
then a thick layer of the egg prepared as above;
continue working thus in alternate layers till
high enough to look handsome. It should be
piled in the form of a cone, and the egg should
form the last layer. It must then be placed in
a gentle oven till it becomes a little set, and the
last layer slightly crisp; a few minutes will
effect this. It must be served in the dish in which
it is baked, and is generally ornamented with
myrtle and gold and silver leaf.

BOLA TOLIEDO.

Take one pound of butter, and warm it over
the fire with a little milk, then put it into a pan
with one pound of flour, six beaten eggs, a

quarter of a pound of beaten sweet almonds, and
two table-spoonsful of yeast ; make these ingredients into a light paste, and set it before the
fire to rise ; then grease a deep dish, and place
in a layer of the paste, then some egg prepared
as for Bola d'Amor, then slices of citron, and a
layer of egg marmalade, sprinkle each layer
with cinnamon, and fill the dish with alternate
layers.   A rich puff paste should line the dish,
which ought to be deep ; bake in a brisk oven,
after which, sugar clarified with orange flour-
water must be poured over till the syrup has
thoroughly penetrated the Bola.

———

A BOLA D'HISPANIOLA.

Take one pound and a half of flour, with three
spoonsful of yeast, two ounces of fresh butter,
one table spoonful of essence of lemon, eight
eggs, and half a tea-cup full of water, and make
it into a light dough, set it to rise for about an
hour, then roll it out and cut it into three
pieces ; have previously ready, a quarter of a
pound of citron, and three quarters of a pound
of orange and lemon peel, cut in thin slices,
mixed with powdered sugar and cinnamon ; the

Bola should be formed with the pieces of dough, layers of the fruit being placed between; it should not be baked in a tin. Powdered sweet almonds and sugar, should be strewed over it before baking.

SUPERIOR RECEIPT FOR ALMOND PUDDING.

Beat up the yolks of ten eggs, and the whites of seven; add half a pound of sweet almonds pounded finely, half a pound of white sugar, half an ounce of bitter almonds, and a tablespoonful of orange flower water, when thoroughly mixed, grease a dish, put in the pudding and bake in a brisk oven; when done, strew powdered sugar over the top, or, which is exceedingly fine, pour over clarified sugar with orange flower water.

GERMAN OR SPANISH PUFFS.

Put a quarter of a pound of fresh butter, and a tea-cup full of cold water into a saucepan, when the butter is melted, stir in, while on the fire, four table spoonsful of flour; when thoroughly mixed, put it in a dish to cool, and then

add four well beaten eggs; butter some cups,
half fill them with the batter, bake in a quick
oven and serve with clarified sugar.

A LUCTION, OR A RACHAEL.

Make a thin nouilles paste, cut into strips of
about two inches wide, leave it to dry, then boil
the strips in a little water, and drain through a
cullender; when the water is strained off, mix
it with beaten eggs, white sugar, a little fresh
butter, and grated lemon peel; bake or boil in
a shape lined with preserved cherries, when
turned out pour over a fine custard, or cream,
flavored with brandy, and sweetened to taste.

PRENESAS.

Take one pint of milk, stir in as much flour as
will bring it to the consistency of hasty pudding;
boil it till it becomes thick, let it cool, and beat
it up with ten eggs; when smooth, take a spoonful at a time, and drop it into a frying-pan, in
which there is a good quantity of boiling clarified
butter, fry of a light brown, and serve with
clarified sugar, flavored with lemon essence.

SOPA D'ORO : OR GOLDEN SOUP.

Clarify a pound of sugar in a quarter of a pint of water, and the same quantity of orange flower-water; cut into pieces the size of dice a thin slice of toasted bread, or cut it into shapes with a paste cutter, throw it, while hot, into the sugar, with an ounce of sweet almonds pounded very finely, then take the beaten yolks of four eggs. Pour over the sugar and bread, stir gently, and let it simmer a few minutes. Serve in a deep glass dish, sprinkled over with pounded cinnamon.

POMMES FRITES.

This is a simple but very nice way of preparing apples. Peel and cut five fine apples in half, dip them in egg and white powdered sugar, and fry in butter; when done, strew a little white sugar over them.

CHEJADOS.

Clarify a pound of sugar in half a pint of water; peel and grate a moderately sized cocoa nut, add it to the syrup, and let it simmer till perfectly soft, putting rose water occasionally to prevent its becoming too dry; stir it continually to prevent burning. Let it cool, and mix it with the beaten yolks of six eggs; make a thin nouilles pastry, cut it into rounds of the size of a tea-cup; pinch up the edges deep enough to form a shape, fill them with the sweet meat, and bake of a light brown. A rich puff paste may be substituted for the nouilles pastry if preferred.

COCOA NUT DOCE.

This is merely the cocoa nut and sugar prepared as above, without egg, and served in small glasses, or baked.

COCOA NUT PUDDING.

Take about half a pound of finely grated cocoa nut; beat up to a cream half a pound of fresh butter, add it to the cocoa nut, with half a pound of white sugar, and six whites of eggs beaten to a froth; mix the whole well together, and bake in a dish lined with a rich puff paste.

EGG MARMALADE.

Clarify one pound of sugar in half a pint of water till it becomes a thick syrup. While clarifying, add one ounce of sweet almonds blanched and pounded; let it cool, and stir in gently the yolks of twenty eggs which have been previously beaten and passed through a sieve; great care must be taken to stir it continually the same way; when well mixed, place it over a slow fire till it thickens, stirring all the time to prevent burning. Some cooks add vanilla, considering the flavor an improvement.

MACROTES.

Take one pound of French roll dough, six ounces of fresh butter, two eggs, and as much flour as will be requisite to knead it together; roll in into the form of a long French roll, and cut it in thin round slices; set them at a short distance from the fire to rise, and then fry in the best Florence oil; when nearly cold, dip them in clarified sugar, flavored with essence of lemon.

TART DE MOY.

Soak three-quarters of a pound of savoy biscuits in a quart of milk; add six ounces of fresh butter, four eggs, one ounce of candid orange peel, the same quantity of lemon peel, and one ounce of citron, mix all well together; sweeten with white sugar, and bake in a quick oven; when nearly done, spread over the top the whites of the eggs well whisked, and return it to the oven.

GRIMSTICH.

Make into a stiff paste one pint of biscuit powder, a little brown sugar, grated lemon peel, six eggs, and three-quarters of a pound of warmed fresh butter; then prepare four apples chopped finely, a quarter of a pound of sweet almonds blanched and chopped, half a pound of stoned raisins, a little nutmeg grated, half a pound of coarse brown sugar, and a glass of white wine, or a little brandy; mix the above ingredients together, and put them on a slow fire to simmer for half an hour, and place in a dish to cool; make the paste into the form of small dumplings, fill them with the fruit, and bake them; when put in the oven, pour over a syrup of brown sugar and water, flavored with lemon juice.

FRENCH ROLL FRITTERS.

Take off the crust of a long round French roll; cut the crumb in thin slices, soak them in boiling milk, taking care they do not break; have a dish ready with several eggs beaten up, and with a fish slice remove the bread from the milk, letting the milk drain off, dip them into the dish of eggs, and half fry them in fine salad oil, they must then be again soaked in the milk and dipped the egg, and then fried of a handsome light brown; while hot, pour over clarified sugar, flavored with cinnamon and orange flower water.

HAMAN'S FRITTERS.

Take two spoonful of the best Florence oil, scald it, and when hot, mix with it one pound of flour, add four beaten eggs and make it into a paste, roll it out thin and cut it into pieces about four inches square, let them dry and fry them in oil; the moment the pieces are put in

the frying pan, they must be drawn up with two
silver skewers into different forms according to
fancy; a few minutes is sufficient to fry them,
they should be crisp when done.

WAFLERS.

Mix a cup and a half of thick yeast with a
little warm milk, and set it with two pounds of
flour before the fire to rise, then mix with them
one pound of fresh butter, ten eggs, a grated
nutmeg, a quarter of a pint of orange flower-
water, a little powdered cinnamon, and three
pints of warm milk; when the batter is perfectly
smooth, butter the irons, fill them with it, close
them down tightly, and put them between the
bars of a bright clear fire; when sufficiently
done, they will slip easily out of the irons.

Wafler irons are required and can be obtained
at any good ironmongers of the Hebrew
persuasion.

LAMPLICH.

Take half a pound of currants, the same
quantity of raisins and sugar, a little citron,
ground cloves and cinnamon, with eight apples

finely chopped; mix all together, then have
ready a rich puff paste cut into small triangles,
fill them with the fruit like puffs, and lay them
in a deep dish, let the pieces be placed closely,
and when the dish is full, pour over one ounce
of fresh butter melted in a tea-cup full of clarified sugar, flavoured with essence of lemon, and
bake in an oven not too brisk.

STAFFIN.

This is composed of the fruit, &c., prepared
as above, but the dish is lined with the paste,
and the fruit laid in alternate layers with paste
till the dish is filled; the paste must form the
top layer, clarified sugar is poured over before it
is put into the oven.

RICE FRITTERS.

Boil half a pound of rice, in a small quantity
of water, to a jelly; let it cool, and beat it up
with six eggs, three spoonsful of flour, a little
grated lemon peel, fry like fritters, either in
butter or oil, and serve with white sugar sifted
over them.

LEMON TART.

Grate the peel of six lemons, add the juice of one, with a quarter of a pound of pounded almonds, a quarter of a pound of preserved lemon and orange peel, half a pound of powdered white sugar, and six eggs well beaten, mix all together, and bake in a dish lined with a fine pastry.

ANOTHER WAY.

Slice six lemons and lay them in sugar all night, then mix with them two savoy biscuits, three ounces of orange and lemon peel, three ounces of ground almonds, one ounce of whole almonds blanched, and bake in a dish lined with pastry. Orange tarts are prepared in the same way, substituting oranges for the lemons.

ALMOND RICE.

Boil half a pound of whole rice in milk until soft, beat it through a sieve, set it on the fire, with sugar according to taste, a few pounded sweet almonds and a few slices of citron; when it has simmered a short time, let it cool; place it it in a mould, and when sufficiently firm turn it out, stick it with blanched almonds, and pour over a fine custard. This may be made without milk, and by increasing the quantity of almonds will be found exceedingly good.

———

ALMOND PASTE.

Blanch half a pound of fine almonds, pound them to a paste, a few drops of water are necessary to be added, from time to time, or they become oily ; then mix thoroughly with it half a pound of white sifted sugar, put it into a preserving pan, and let them simmer very gently until they become dry enough not to stick to a clean spoon when touched; it must be constantly stirred.

———

RICE FRUIT TARTS.

For persons who dislike pastry, the following is an excellent way of preparing fruit. Boil in milk some whole rice till perfectly soft, sweeten with white sugar, and when nearly cold, line a dish with it, have ready some currants, raspberries, cherries, or any other fruit, which must have been previously stewed and sweetened, fill the dish with it; beat up the whites of three eggs to a froth, mixed with a little white sugar, and lay over the top, and place it in the oven for half an hour,

BREAD FRUIT TARTS.

Line a dish with thin slices of bread, then lay the fruit with brown sugar in alternate layers, with slices of bread; when the dish is filled, pour over half a tea-cup full of water, and let the top be formed of thin pieces of bread thickly strewed over with brown sugar, bake until thoroughly done.

RICE CUSTARD.

This is a very innocent and nutritive custard. Take two ounces of whole rice and boil it in three pints of milk until it thickens, then add half a pound of pounded sweet almonds, and sweeten to taste; a stick of cinnamon and a piece of lemon peel should be boiled in it, and then taken out.

CREME BRUN.

Boil a large cup of cream, flavor with essence of almonds and cinnamon, and then mix with

it the yolk of three eggs, carefully beaten and
strained, stirring one way to keep it smooth;
place it on a dish in small heaps, strew over
powdered sugar and beaten almonds, and brown
with a salamander.

PANCAKES.

Mix a light batter of eggs with flour and milk
or water, fry in boiling butter or clarified suet;
they may be fried without butter or fat, by
putting more eggs and a little cream, the pan
must be very dry and clean; those fried without
butter are very delicate and fashionable, they
should be fried of the very lightest colour;
they are good also made of rice, which must be
boiled in milk till quite tender; then beat up
with eggs, and flavoured according to taste,
and fried like other pancakes.

PANCAKES FOR CHILDREN.

Take a pint of finely grated bread crumbs,
simmer in a little milk and water, flavour with
cinnamon or lemon peel grated, add a couple of

K

beaten eggs, and sweeten to taste, drop a small quantity into the pan and fry like pancakes.

A NICE RICE PUDDING FOR CHILDREN.

Boil till tender half a pound of well picked rice in one quart of fresh milk, sweeten with white sugar, and flavour with whole cinnamon, lemon peel, and a bay leaf; when the rice is tender, place it in a deep dish, pour over a very little butter warmed in a little milk, and bake until brown; a slow oven is requisite unless the rice is extremely soft before it is put in the oven.

A RICH BREAD AND BUTTER PUDDING.

Lay in a deep dish alternate layers of bread and butter cut from a French roll, and the following mixture: the yolks of four eggs beaten, four ounces of moist sugar, a few soaked ratafias, a table-spoonful of brandy and a few currants; fill up the dish with these layers, and pour over a little milk, the last layer should be of bread and butter, the whites of the eggs beaten to a froth may, if an elegant appearance is wished for, be laid over the top when the pudding is nearly baked.

___

A CHERRY BATTER PUDDING.

Stone and pick some fine cherries, put them into a buttered mould, and pour over them a fine batter well sweetened, tie over the mould closely, and boil one hour and a half; serve with sweet sauce.   This is a delicious pudding; plums or damsons are sometimes used instead of cherries.

___

CUMBERLAND PUDDING.

Take equal quantities of bread crumbs, apples finely chopped, currants and shred suet, sweeten with brown sugar, and mix all together with three eggs, a little brandy, grated nutmeg, and lemon peel; boil in a round mould from one to two hours, according to the size of the pudding.

___

COLLEGE PUDDING.

These are made in a similar way to Cumberland pudding, with the omission of the apples, they are made in balls, and fried or baked in cups.   A sweet sauce is served with them.

PLUM PUDDING.

To one pound of currants add one pound of raisins, one pound of shred suet, one pound flour (or half a pound bread crumbs and half a pound of flour), a quarter of a pound of candied orange and lemon peel, a little citron cut thin, half a pound of moist sugar; mix all well together as each article is added, then stir in six beaten eggs and a glass of brandy, beat the pudding well for half an hour, let it stand some time, then put it into a basin and boil six or seven hours in plenty of water; it should be seasoned according to taste with ginger, nutmeg, cloves, &c. Serve with sifted sugar or whites of eggs beaten to a froth.

RATAFIA PUDDING.

Soak the crumb of a French roll and half a pound of ratafia cakes in milk or cream, then mix with them three ounces of warmed fresh butter, the yolks of five and the whites of two eggs, sweeten to taste; add one ounce of pounded almonds, and a few bitter almonds, boil in a shape lined with dried cherries, or bake in a cake-tin first well buttered, and sprinkled with bread crumbs.

PASSOVER PUDDING.

Mix equal quantities of biscuit powder and shred suet, half the quantity of currants and raisins, a little spice and sugar, with an ounce of candied peels, and fine well beaten eggs; make these into a stiff batter, and boil well, and serve with a sweet sauce. This pudding is excellent baked in a pudding tin, it must be turned out when served.

ANOTHER SORT.

Mix the various ingredients above-named, substituting for the raisins, apples minced finely, add a larger proportion of sugar, and either boil or bake.

ANOTHER SORT.

Mix into a batter a cup full of biscuit powder, with a little milk and a couple of eggs, to which add three ounces of sugar, two of warmed butter, a little shred of lemon peel, and a tablespoonful of rum; pour the mixture into a mould, and boil or bake.

PASSOVER FRITTERS.

Mix into a smooth batter a tea-cup of biscuit powder with beaten eggs, and sweeten with white sifted sugar; add grated lemon peel, and a spoonful of orange flower-water, and fry of a light brown; the flavor may be varied by substituting a few beaten almonds, with one or two bitter, instead of the orange flower-water.

A SUPERIOR RECEIPT FOR PASSOVER FRITTERS.

Make a thin batter as already described in the former receipt; drop it into a souflé pan, fry lightly, and strew over pounded cinnamon, sifted sugar, and finely chopped almonds; hold over a salamander to brown the upper side. Slide the fritter on to a hot dish, and fold; pour over, when in the dish, clarified sugar.

PASSOVER CURRANT FRITTERS.

Mix a thick batter, as before, add some well-washed and dried currants, and fry of a rich brown; serve with a sweet sauce, flavored with wine or shrub, and sweetened with moist sugar; these are often made in the shape of small balls, and fried and served in the same sauce.

BATTER PUDDING.

Stir in three ounces of flour, four beaten eggs, and one pint of milk, sweeten to taste, and mix to a smooth batter about the thickness of good cream, and boil in a buttered basin.

CUSTARD PUDDING.

To one desert spoonful of flour, add one pint of fresh milk and the yolks of five eggs; flavor according to fancy, with sugar, nutmeg, or lemon-peel; beat to a froth two whites of eggs and pour to the rest; boil rather more than half an hour.

BREAD PUDDING.

Grate stale bread, or soak the crumb of a French roll in milk, which must be warmed; beat with it two or three eggs, flavor and sweeten to taste, sometimes with a little wine or essence of lemon, or beaten almonds; it will require to be boiled about half an hour. This pudding is excellent made as above, with the addition of the peel of one whole lemon grated, with its juice, and baked.

———

VERMICELLI AND MACCARONI PUDDING.

Boil till tender four ounces of either of the above articles, in a pint of milk; flavor as directed in the preceding receipt, and boil in a mould, which may be lined with raisins. It should be served with any sweet pudding sauce.

———

MILLET, ARROWROOT, GROUND RICE, RICE, TAPIOCA, AND SAGO PUDDINGS.

Puddings of this sort are so similar and simple, that it is only necessary to give one receipt, which will serve as a guide for all;—they are all made with milk, all require to be thoroughly done, all require to be mixed with eggs and sweetened with sugar, and are good either boiled or baked. The cook must use her judgment in adopting the quantities to the size of the pud-

ding required, and the taste of the family she
serves.

––––

MINCED MEAT.

Take one pound of tender roasted meat, two
pounds of shred suet, three pounds of currants,
six chopped apples, a quarter of a loaf grated,
nutmegs, cloves, pepper, salt, one pound of
sugar, grated lemon and orange peel, lemon juice,
and two wine glasses of brandy, the same of
white wine, and two ounces of citron, and the
same of candied lemon peel; mix all well
together; the ingredients ought to be added
separately. Minced meat should be kept a
day or two before using. The same proportions,
as above, without meat, will be very good; a
little port wine is sometimes substituted for the
brandy.

––––

BAKED SUET PUDDING.

Mix one pint of water, six ounces of flour,
three of shred suet, and two or three beaten
eggs; sweeten to taste. Add raisins or currants
if approved, and bake in a brick oven.

YORKSHIRE PUDDING.

Mix into a smooth batter half a pound of flour, four eggs, if intended to be rich, otherwise two, a pint of milk, and a little salt, it should be about an inch thick; it can be made with or without milk by using a greater proportion of eggs, but it is not so good.

GATEAU DE TOURS.

Take a pound-cake, cut it in slices about half an inch in thickness, spread each slice with jam or preserve, then replace them to the original form; cover the cake with whites of eggs and sugar, whisked to a froth, and set it in a cool oven to dry.

JAUMANGE.

Simmer half a pound of white sugar in three-quarters of a pint of water, with the thinly cut peel of two lemons; when the sugar is melted, add an ounce of dissolved isinglass, and the juice of three lemons, a glass of brandy and three of sherry, beat up with this the yolks of five or

six eggs. Place the basin in which it is mixed
into a pan of boiling water to thicken it, then
pour it into a mould and set it to cool; if it
does not thicken by being put in a pan of boiling water, set the pan on the fire and stir it
for a few minutes.

GATEAU DE POMME.

Take ten or twelve fine baking apples, peel
and take out the cores, and let them simmer in
milk and water; when soft drain them, and beat
them up with a wooden fork, with half an ounce of
dissolved isinglass, white sifted sugar, sufficient
to sweeten, and grated lemon peel. Put the
mixture, when perfectly smooth, into a mould,
set it in ice or a very cool place, when it is
turned out it should be covered with a fine
custard.

APPLE CHARLOTTE.

Prepare the apples as in the last receipt; but
instead of using a jelly mould, put the apples into
an oval cake tin about the size of a small side dish,
four or five inches high; when cold, turn it out

and cover the apple-shape with savoy cakes placed closely together perpendicularly; all round the top of the charlotte should be covered with whites of eggs and sugar, beaten to a stiff froth, and placed in small balls; a salamander should be used to crisp them and to give a slight peach-like colour; a tasteful cook will, after crisping the first layer of these balls, add others over them to form a sort of cone high in the centre, that will have a pretty effect if well done. This is an easy and elegant *entremét*, and by no means an expensive one.

A SOUFLE.

Take half a pint of cream and the same quantity of new milk, and warm them together in a clean saucepan, meanwhile make a smooth batter with four ounces of rice-flour or potatoe-flour, and stir into the milk, let it simmer, stirring all the time till it thickens; then add two to three ounces of fresh butter, and white sifted sugar enough to sweeten, and a little grated lemon peel; then take it off the fire and stir quickly to it the well-beaten yolks of six to eight eggs, butter the pan and pour the

mixture into it, when on the point of being
placed into the oven, add the whites of the
eggs thoroughly whisked; the pan must be only
half filled, as it will rise very high; it must be
served immediately it is taken from the oven,
even in passing to the dinner table a salamander
should be held over it, to prevent its falling and
becoming heavy and unsightly.   The French
flavour a souflé with orange flour-water or
vanilla, and the rind of a Seville orange is sometimes substituted for the rind of a lemon ; there
are dishes made expressly for souflés.

A PLAIN SOUFLE.

Mix well together six ounces of rice-flour,
arrowroot, or *tous les mois*, with half a pint of
milk flavoured with essence of almond and
lemon peel, or orange-flour water, let it thicken
over the fire, stirring to keep it smooth, sweeten
with white sugar, add the beaten yolks of five
eggs, proceed as in the last receipt, adding the
whisked whites at the moment of placing the
souflé into the oven ; if there happen to be no
souflé dish, a cake-tin may make a tolerable
substitute, a paper fringed should then line the

tin and a napkin should be twisted round it
when brought to table.

___

A SWEET OMELET.

Beat up three or four eggs, pour them into
an omelet pan, and sprinkle a little white sugar
over them while frying, hold a salamander or
hot shovel over the uppermost side of the omelet,
as it must only be fried on one side. As soon
as it is set, slide it on to a hot dish, double it,
and sprinkle sugar over it and serve quickly.

___

OMLETTE SOUFLEE.

Fry the eggs as directed for sweet omelet,
using about five yolks and two whites, all of
which require being finely beaten and strained.
Soften a little preserve by holding it over the
fire, or mixing a little warm water with it,
spread it slightly over the omelette, have the
remainder of the whites whisked to a froth with
white sugar, and lay it on the preserve; slide the
omelette on to a hot dish, double it, and serve
directly.

FANCY CREAMS.

Put into a basin a pint of cream, to which add four ounces of powdered white sugar, and the rind of a lemon rubbed on a lump of sugar, and a glass of sherry wine; whisk them well and mix with it half an ounce of dissolved isinglass, beat it all thoroughly together, and fill the mould, which should be set in ice till wanted. A table spoonful of marasquino added to the above, will make *Italian cream*. A table spoonful of fresh or preserved pine-apple will make *pine-apple cream;* this will require the addition of a little lemon syrup. A table spoonful of ratafia, will make it *ratifia cream.*

The juice of strawberries or raspberries make fine fruit creams; *mille fruit cream* is made by mixing with the cream any kind of small preserved fruit.

RICE SOUFLES.

Boil well some fine picked rice, in pure fresh milk, sweeten and flavour with a bay leaf, lemon peel, and a stick of cinnamon, all which must be taken out when the rice is done, then line

with it a round dish, or soufflé dish, have ready
apples previously boiled, sweetened, and beat
up smoothly, place the apple lightly in the
centre rather higher in the middle than at the
sides, beat up the whites of eggs to a froth,
sweeten and flavour with lemon, or noyau
essence; place it in small heaps tastefully on
the apple and rice, and brown delicately with
a salamander. This soufflé may have stewed
cherries or any *other* kind of fruit, instead of the
apples if preferred.

BOILED CUSTARD.

Take a pint of milk, let it simmer in a very
clean saucepan, flavor it with lemon-peel and a
bay leaf, and sweeten to taste; while gently
boiling, add the beaten yolks of four eggs, and
the whites of two, continue stirring until the
custard thickens, when it must be removed
from the fire, but it is requisite to stir it until
it cools. It is necessary to strain the milk
before the eggs are added, and also to pass the
eggs through a sieve. Custards are flavoured
sometimes with essence of almonds; a little
cream added to the milk is a great improvement.

The above mixture may be baked in small cups; they require a quarter of an hour to bake.

CALF'S FEET JELLY.

Boil two feet in two quarts, or five pints of water, till the water has half wasted; strain, and when cold, take off the fat, then put it in the saucepan with lump sugar, lemon juice, and white wine to taste, also a little lemon peel; when simmered a few minutes, throw in the whites of two eggs, and their shells broken, which will have the effect of clarifying the jelly; let it boil about ten minutes after the scum rises, then pour it through a flannel bag or thick cloth, dipping the bag or cloth first into hot water; pass the jelly through it until clear, then pour it into moulds and put them in a cool place to set. One calf's foot and one cow heel will be more economical than two calf's feet. If fruit is desired to be in the jelly, it must be put in when the jelly begins to stiffen in the mould.

L

ORANGE JELLY.

This can be made with calf's feet or without. One quart of water will require one ounce of isinglass, simmer the isinglass in the water, and add the peel of one lemon and one orange ; when the isinglass is dissolved, add the juice of a lemon and six fine oranges ; although the quantity must vary according to the season for them, sweeten with half a pound of white sugar : a Seville orange is added if there should not be much flavor in the others.

Lemon jelly is made in the same way ; the peel of a Seville orange and of a lemon is used, with the juice of five lemons ; rather more sugar will be required with this jelly than with the former.

Punch jelly is made in the same way. An equal quantity of brandy and rum, with the juice of two or three lemons is mixed with the isinglass, which is dissolved in one pint of water, the other pint of liquid being made up by the lemon juice and spirits.

The essence of noyeau is reckoned to give an exquisite flavor, in this case it requires to be coloured with a few drops of cochineal.

AN EASY TRIFLE.

Soak three sponge cakes and half a pound of macaroons and ratafias in one wine glass of brandy and three of white wine, lay them at the bottom of the trifle dish, and pour over nearly a pint of thick rich custard, made of equal portions of milk and cream, with seven eggs, according to directions for " Custards;" before the custard is added, jam and sweetmeats are sometimes spread over the cakes; a fine light froth is prepared with cream and the whites of two eggs, flavored with wine and sugar, heap it over the trifle lightly.

A STILL MORE SIMPLE ONE, AND QUICKLY MADE.

Soak ratafia cakes in wine, with a little brandy; pour over a thick custard, and cover with a froth of the white of eggs, flavored with wine and sweetened with white sugar.

BLANCMANGE.

To a quart of milk add half an ounce of fine isinglass, a handful of beaten almonds, and two or three bitter almonds, a couple of bay leaves, and a piece of lemon peel; when the isinglass is dissolved, strain the milk into a basin; sweeten with four ounces of white sugar, and pour into a mould.

The juice of fresh strawberries is a fine addition to blancmange.

A JUDITHA.

Put some gooseberries into a saucepan with very little water, when they are soft, pulp them through a sieve, and add several well-beaten yolks of eggs, and sweeten with white sugar; have ready a shape of biscuit ice, or any other cream ice that may be preferred, take off a thick slice of the ice from the top carefully, and without breaking, so that it may be replaced on the ice. Scoop out a large portion of the ice which may be mixed with the gooseberry cream, and fill the hollow with it. Cover the shape with the piece that was removed and serve. This is an elegant dish, the ice should be prepared in a round mould—brown-bread ice is particularly well adapted to a Juditha.

TOURTE A LA CRÊME.

This is a fashionable and delicate description of tart. A couple of round cutters about the size of a pie plate are required for it, one of the cutters must be about two inches smaller than the other, if they are fluted the tourte will have a better appearance.

Roll out some very rich puff paste to the thickness of one inch, and cut two pieces with the larger tin cutter, then press the smaller cutter through one of these pieces, and remove the border which will be formed round it; this must be laid very evenly upon the other piece of paste, and slightly pressed to make it adhere; place the tourte in an oven to bake for about twenty minutes, then let it become cool, but not cold, and fill it with a fine custard or with any rich preserves; if the latter, a well whipped cream may be laid lightly over; the pastry may be glazed if approved.

THE GROSVENOR PUDDING.

Beat half a pound of butter with the same quantity of white sugar until it is like cream, then beat up five eggs and add them with half a pound of flour, a quarter of a pound of currants, two ounces of candied orange and lemon peel cut in thin slices, and a few drops of lemon essence; when these ingredients are well mixed and beaten, butter a pudding tin, pour in the mixture, and bake in a moderately quick oven.

CITRON PUDDING.

Cut in slices two ounces of citron, the same quantity of candied orange and lemon peel, add to them four ounces of loaf sugar, and four of fresh butter; line a dish with fine puff paste, and beat up to a froth the yolks of four eggs and the whites of two, fill the dish with these ingredients and bake half an hour. The dish should be shallow.

STEWED PEARS.

Peel, core, and quarter a dozen fine large baking pears, put them into a stewpan with half a pound of white sugar and sufficient cold water to cover them; with a small quantity of the peelings, a few cloves, and a little cochineal tied up

in a muslin bag, let them stew gently, and
closely covered until tender.

BAKED PEARS.

Peel them and stick a couple of cloves in
each pear, place them in a deep dish, with half
a pound of brown sugar and a little water, let
them bake till quite tender.

STEWED PIPPINS.

Peel the pippins and stew them gently with
a little water, white sugar, and a little lemon
peel; preserve is usually used to ornament the
top of each apple; they should, when done,
look white and rather transparent.

SIESTA CAKE.

Take one pound of butter, warm it over the
fire with a little milk, put it into a pan with a
pound of flour, six eggs, a quarter of a pound of
sweet almonds finely pounded, and two table-
spoonsful of yeast; beat these ingredients well
together into a light paste, and set it before the
fire to rise, butter the inside of a pan, and fill

it with alternate layers of the paste, and of
pounded almonds, sugar, citron, and cinnamon;
when baked, and while hot, make holes through
the siesta with a small silver skewer, taking care
not to break it, and pour over clarified sugar till
it is perfectly soaked through.

A PLAIN BOLA.

Take three quarters of a pound of white
sugar, three quarters of a pound of fresh butter,
two eggs, one pound and a half of flour, three
spoonsful of yeast, a little milk, and two ounces
of citron cut thin, and mix into a light paste;
bake in a tin, and strew powdered sugar and
cinnamon over it before baking.

The above ingredients are often baked in
small tins or cups.

ALMOND TEA-CAKES.

Take half-a-pound of flour, three ounces of
which are to be put aside for rolling out the
cakes, the other five ounces, with a quarter of a
pound of fresh butter, are to be set before the
fire for a few minutes; after which mix with it

half a pound of sugar, a quarter of a pound of
sweet almonds, chopped fine, and a couple of
eggs; make these ingredients into thin cakes,
and strew over them ground almonds and white
sugar, and bake in a brisk oven.

OIL TWIST.

Take half a quartern of dough, one gill of
the best Florence oil, half a pound of currants,
half a pound of moist sugar, and a little cinnamon; mix all well together, make it up in the
form of a twist, and bake it.

CINNAMON CAKES.

Rub half a pound of fresh butter into a
pound of flour; work it well together, then add
half a pound of sifted sugar, and a tea-spoonful
of pounded cinnamon, and make it into a paste,
with three eggs; roll it, and cut into small
cakes, with tin cutters.

RICH PLUM CAKE.

Beat to a cream one pound of butter, to
which add the same quantity of sifted loaf

sugar and of fine flour, the whites of ten eggs beaten to a froth, and the yolks of the same also beaten till quite smooth and thin, and half a nutmeg grated; lastly, work in one pound of well-washed currants, half a pound of mixed candied peels, cut small, and a glass of brandy; bake for two hours.

DIET-BREAD CAKE.

Beat together five eggs and half a pound of white sugar, then add six ounces of flour well dried and sifted, a little lemon-juice and grated lemon-peel; bake in a moderate oven.

DROP CAKES.

Mix one pound of flour with the same quantity of butter, sugar, and currants; make these into a paste with a couple of eggs, add a little orange flower-water and a little white wine; if the paste is likely to be too thin when two eggs are used, omit the white of one; drop the mixture when ready on a tin plate, and bake.

A COMMON CAKE.

Rub in with one pound of flour six ounces of butter, and two tea-spoonsful of yeast, to a paste; set it to rise, then mix in five eggs, half a pound of sugar, and a quarter of a pint of milk; add currants or carraways, and beat well together.   If required to be richer, put more butter and eggs, and add candied citron and lemon-peel.

A SODA CAKE.

Mix with the above ingredients one drachm of soda, which should be rubbed in with the flour.   This is reckoned a wholesome cake, and half the quantity of eggs are required, or it may be rendered a fine rich cake by increasing the quantity of eggs, butter, and fruit.

A PLAIN CAKE.

Work into two pounds of dough a quarter of a pound of sugar, the same of butter; add a couple of eggs, and bake in a tin.

A POUND CAKE.

Beat to cream a pound of butter and a pound of sifted loaf sugar; add eight beaten eggs, stir in lightly three quarters of a pound of flour, beat well together, and bake for one hour in a brisk oven; currants may be added if approved.

BUTTER CAKES.

Take equal quantities of butter and sugar, say half a pound of each, grate the rind of a lemon, add a little cinnamon, and as much flour as will form it into a paste, with spice and eggs; roll it out, cut it into two small cakes, and bake. A piece of candied orange or lemon-peel may be put on the top of each cake.

LITTLE SHORT CAKES.

Rub into a pound of flour four ounces of butter, four ounces of white powdered sugar, and two eggs; make it into a paste, roll it thin, and cut into small cakes with tin cutters.

A little orange flower-water or sweet wine improve the flavour of these cakes.

MATSO CAKES.

Make a stiff paste with biscuit powder and milk and water; add a little butter, the yolk of an egg, and a little white sugar; cut into pieces, and mould with the hand, and bake in a brisk oven. These cakes should not be too thin.

ANOTHER SORT.

Warm a quarter of a pint of water flavoured with a little salt, in which mix four beaten eggs; then mix half a pound of matso flour, and a couple of lumps of white sugar, and half a tea-cup of milk; mix all well together, and bake in a tin.

FRIED MATSOS.

Soak some of the thickest matsos in milk, taking care they do not break; then fry in boiling fresh butter. This is a very nice method of preparing them for breakfast or tea.

MATSO DIET BREAD.

Simmer one pound of white sugar in a quarter of a pint of water, which pour hot upon eight well-beaten eggs; beat till cold, when add one pound of matso flour, a little grated lemon-peel, and bake in a papered tin, or in small tins; the cake must be removed while hot.

A CAKE WITHOUT BUTTER.

Beat well five eggs, to which add six ounces of flour; flavour with beaten almonds, and add, if liked, thin slices of citron; bake in a mould in a moderate oven.

SPONGE CAKES.

Mix six eggs, half the whites, half a pound of lump sugar, half a pound of flour, and a quarter of a pint of water, which should be strongly flavoured by lemon peel having been in it for some hours; the sugar and water should boil up together, and poured over the eggs after they have been well whisked, which must be continued while the liquid is being poured over them, and until they become quite thick and white, then stir in the flour, which must be warm and dry. Pour the mixture into a couple of cake tins, and bake in a gentle oven.

A NICE BREAKFAST CAKE.

Make a paste of half a pound of flour, one ounce of butter, a very little salt, two eggs, and a table-spoonful of milk, roll it out, but first set it to rise before the fire; cut it into cakes the size of small cheese plates, sprinkle with flour, and bake on a tin in a brisk oven, or they may be fried in a clean frying pan; they should be cut in half, buttered hot, and served quickly.

ICING FOR CAKES.

Whisk half a pound of sifted white sugar, with one wine glass of orange flower-water, and the whites of two eggs, well beaten and strained; it must be whisked until it is quite thick and white; and when the cake is almost cold, dip a soft camel's hair brush into it, and cover the cake well, and set it in a cool oven to harden.

TO CLARIFY SUGAR.

Take the proportion of one pound of sugar to half a pint of water, with the whites of a couple of eggs; boil it up twice, then set it by for the impurities to rise to the top, and skim it carefully.

CHAPTER VIII.

Preserving and Bottling.

————

ATTENTION and a little practice will ensure excellence in such preserves as are in general use
in private families; and it will always be found
a more economical plan to purchase the more
rare and uncommon articles of preserved fruits
than to have them made at home.

The more sugar that is added to fruit the less
boiling it requires.

If jellies be over-boiled, much of the sugar
will become candied, and leave the jelly thin.

Every thing used for the purpose of preserving
should be clean and very dry, particularly bottles for bottled fruit.

Fruit should boil rapidly *before* the sugar is

M

added, and quietly afterwards—when preserves seem likely to become mouldy, it is generally a sign they have not been sufficiently boiled, and it will be requisite to boil them up again—fruit for bottling should not be too ripe, and should be perfectly fresh; there are various methods adopted by different cooks : the fruit may be placed in the bottles, and set in a moderate oven until considerably shrunken, when the bottles should be removed and closely corked; or the bottles may be set in a pan with cold water up to the necks, placed over the fire ; when the fruit begins to sink remove them, and when cold fill up each bottle with cold spring water, cork the bottles, and lay them on their sides in a dry place.

To bottle red currants—pick them carefully from the stalk, and add, as the currants are put in, sifted white sugar ; let the bottles be well filled and rosin the corks, and keep them with their necks downwards.

BRANDIED CHERRIES.

Put into a large wide mouthed bottle very ripe black cherries, add to them two pounds of loaf sugar, a quart of brandy, and a few cloves, then bruise a few more cherries, and simmer with sugar, strain and add the juice to the cherries in the bottle, cork closely, and keep in a warm dry place.

QUINCE MARMALADE.

Peel, cut into quarters, and core two pounds of sharp apples, and the same quantity of quinces; put them into a jar, with one pound of white sugar powdered and sprinkled over them; cover them with half a pint of water, and put in also a little bruised cochineal tied in a muslin. Set them in a slack oven till tender, take out the cochineal, and pulp the fruit to a marmalade.

Some cooks prefer boiling the sugar and water first and scalding the fruit till tender, and then adding them to the syrup.

DAMSON MARMALADE.

Is made in the same manner as quince, as also apricot marmalade, which is very fine; the fruit must be stoned, and some of the kernels put in with the fruit, which are peeled, and apricots are cut in pieces; they should be carefully pulped through a clean sieve.

———

PRESERVED APRICOTS.

Halve and pare ripe apricots, or if not quite ripe, boil them till the skin can easily be removed. Lay them in a dish hollow downwards, sift over them their own weight of white sugar, let them lay for some hours, then put the fruit, with the sugar and juice into a preserving pan, and simmer till the fruit is clear, take it out, put it carefully into pots, and pour over the syrup.

This receipt will serve as a guide for preserved nectarines, peaches, plums, gages, &c. A few of the kernels should always be put in with the fruit, as they improve the flavor of the preserve.

———

STRAWBERRIES PRESERVED WHOLE.

Weigh an equal quantity of fruit and white sugar powdered, sift all the sugar over the fruit, so that half of it shall equally be covered, let it lay till the next day, when boil the remainder with red currant juice, in which simmer the strawberries until the jelly hangs about them. Put the strawberries into pots, taking care not to break them, and pour over the syrup.

This receipt will serve for raspberries and cherries, which make a fine preserve.

STRAWBERRY JAM.

Bruise gently, with the back of a wooden spoon, six pounds of fine fresh fruit, and boil them with very little water for twenty minutes, stirring until the fruit and juice are well mixed; then put in powdered loaf sugar of equal weight to the fruit, and simmer half an hour longer. If the preserve is not required to be very rich, half the weight of sugar in proportion to the quantity of fruit may be used; but more boiling will be requisite. By this recipe also are made raspberry, currant, gooseberry, apricot, and other jams.

RED CURRANT JELLY.

Strip carefully from the stems some quite ripe currants, put them into a preserving pan, stir them gently over a clear fire until the juice flows freely from them, then squeeze the currants and strain the juice through a folded muslin or jelly bag; pour it into a preserving pan, adding, as it boils, white sugar, in the proportion of one pound of sugar to one pint of juice.

If made with less sugar, more boiling will be required, by which much juice and flavour are lost. A little dissolved isinglass is used by confectioners, but it is much better without. Jams and jellies should be poured into pots when in a boiling state.

Jellies should be continually skimmed till the scum ceases to rise, so that they may be clear and fine. White currant jelly and black are made in the same manner as red. By this receipt can be made raspberry jelly, strawberry jelly, and all other kinds.

APPLE JELLY.

Pare, core, and cut small any kind of fine baking apples—say six pounds in weight; put them in a preserving pan with one quart of water; boil gently till the apples are very soft and broken, then pass the juice through a jelly bag; when, to each pint, add half a pound of loaf sugar, set it on the fire to boil twenty minutes, skimming it as the scum rises; it must not be over boiled, or the colour will be too dark.

PEAR-SYRUP OR JELLY.

This preparation, although little known in England, forms an important article of economy in many parts of the Continent. The pears are first heated in a saucepan over the fire until the pulp, skins, &c., have separated from the juice, which is then strained, and boiled with coarse brown sugar to the thickness of treacle; but it has a far more agreeable flavour. It is cheaper than butter or treacle, and is excellent spread upon bread for children.

PLUM JAM.

This is a useful and cheap preserve. Choose the large long black plum; to each gallon of

which add three pounds of good moist sugar;
bake them till they begin to crack, when, put
them in pots, of a size for once using, as the air
is apt to spoil the jam.

CHAPTER IX.

Pickling.

———

THE best vinegar should always be used for pickling; in all cases it should be boiled and strained.

The articles to be pickled should first be parboiled or soaked in brine, which should have about six ounces of salt to one quart of water.

The spices used for pickling are whole pepper, long peppers, allspice, mace, mustard-seed, and ginger, the last being first bruised.

The following is a good proportion of spice: to one quart of vinegar put half an ounce of ginger, the same quantity of whole-pepper and allspice, and one ounce of mustard-seed; four shalots, and one clove of garlic.

Pickles should be kept secure from the air, or they soon become soft; the least quantity of water, or a wet spoon, put into a jar of pickles, will spoil the contents.

———

TO PICKLE GHERKINS AND FRENCH BEANS.

These are, of all vegetables, the most difficult to pickle, so that their green colour and freshness may be preserved. Choose some fine fresh gherkins, and set them to soak in brine for a week; then drain them, and pour over boiling vinegar, prepared with the usual spices, first having covered them with fresh vine leaves. If they do not appear to be of a fine green, pour off the vinegar, boil it up again, cover the gherkins with fresh green vine leaves, and pour over the vinegar again. French beans are pickled exactly the same.

———

TO PICKLE CAULIFLOWERS.

Remove the stalks and leaves, break the flower into pieces, parboil them in brine, then drain them, and lay them in a jar, and pour over boiling spiced vinegar.

TO PICKLE MELON MANGOES.

Cut the melons in half, remove the pulpy
part and the seeds, soak the halves for a week in
strong brine, then fill them with the usual
spices, mustard-seed and garlic, and tie them
together with packthread; put them in jars,
and pour over boiling spiced vinegar. Large
cucumbers may be pickled in the same way.

PICCALILI.

Pickle gherkins, French beans, and cauliflower, separately, as already directed; the other
vegetables used are carrots, onions, capsicums,
white cabbage, celery, and, indeed almost any
kind may be put into this pickle, except wal-
nuts and red cabbage. They must be cut in
small pieces, and soaked in brine, the carrots
only, requiring to be boiled in it to make them
tender; then prepare a liquor as follows: into
half a gallon of vinegar put two ounces of
ginger, one of whole black pepper, one of whole
allspice, and one of bruised chillies, three
ounces of shalots, and one ounce of garlic; boil
together nearly twenty minutes; mix a little of it

in a basin, with two ounces of flour of mustard
and one ounce of turmeric, and stir it in gradually with the rest; then pour the liquor over
the vegetables.

TO PICKLE MUSHROOMS.

Choose small button mushrooms, clean and
wipe them, and throw them into cold water,
then put into a stewpan with a little salt, and
cover them with distilled vinegar, and simmer a
few minutes. Put them in bottles with a couple
of blades or so of mace, and when cold, cork
them closely.

TO PICKLE ONIONS.

Choose all of a size and soak in boiling brine,
when cold, drain them and put them in bottles,
and fill up with hot distilled vinegar; if they
are to be *white*, use white wine vinegar; if they
are to be *brown*, use the best distilled vinegar,
adding, in both cases, a little mace, ginger, and
whole pepper.

TO PICKLE WHITE AND RED CABBAGE.

Take off the outside leaves, cut out the stalk,
and shred the cabbage into a cullender, sprinkle

with salt, let it remain for twenty-four hours, then drain it. Put it into jars, and fill up with boiling vinegar, prepared with the usual spices ; if the cabbage is red, a little cochineal powdered, or a slice or two of beet-root is necessary to make the pickle a fine colour ; if it is white cabbage, add instead, a little turmeric powder.

TO PICKLE WALNUTS.

Soak in brine for a week, prick them, and simmer in brine, then let them lay on a sieve to drain, and to turn black, after which place them in jars, and pour over boiling spiced vinegar.

AN OLD WAY OF PICKLING CUCUMBERS.

Cut the cucumbers in small pieces, length ways, with the peel left on ; lay them in salt for twenty-four hours, then dry the pieces with a cloth, lay them in a deep dish, and pour over the following mixture : some vinegar boiled with cayenne pepper, whole ginger, a little whole pepper, and mustard seed, a few West India pickles are by some considered an im-

provement.   This mixture should stand till
nearly cold before covering the cucumbers,
which should then be bottled.   This pickle is
fit for eating a few days after it is made, and will
also keep good in a dry place as long as may be
required.

CHAPTER X.

Receipts for Invalids.

BEEF TEA.

Cut one pound of fleshy beef in dice, or thin slices, simmer for a short time without water, to extract the juices, then add, by degrees, one quart of water, a little salt, a piece of lemon peel, and a sprig of parsley, are the only necessary seasonings; if the broth is required to be stronger put less water.

CHICKEN PANADA.

Boil a chicken till rather more than half done in a quart of water, take of the skin, cut off the white parts when cold, and pound it to a paste in a mortar, with a small quantity of the liquor it was boiled in, season with salt, a little nutmeg, and the least piece of lemon peel; boil it gently, and make it with the liquor in which the fowl has been boiled of the required consistency. It should be rather thicker than cream.

CHICKEN BROTH.

After the white parts have been removed for the panada, return the rest of the chicken to the saucepan, with the liquid, add one blade of mace, one slice only of onion, a little salt, and a piece of lemon peel; carefully remove every particle of fat. Vermicelli is very well adapted for this broth.

RESTORATIVE JELLIES.

There are various kinds of simple restorative jellies suited to an invalid, among the best are the following :—

HARTSHORN JELLY.

Boil half a pound of hartshorn shavings in two quarts of water over a gentle fire until it becomes thick enough to hang about a spoon, then strain it into a clean saucepan and add half a pint of sherry wine, and a quarter of a pound of white sugar, clear it by stirring in the whites of a couple of eggs, whisked to a froth; boil it for about four or five minutes, add the juice of three lemons, and stir all together, when it is well curdled, strain it and pour into the mould, if the color is required to be deeper than the wine will make it, a little saffron may be boiled in it.

BARLEY JELLY.

Boil in an iron saucepan, one tea-cup full of pearl barley, with one quart of cold water, pour off the water when it boils, and add another quart, let it simmer very gently for three hours over or near a slow fire, stirring it frequently with a wooden spoon, strain it, and sweeten with white sugar, add the juice of a lemon, a little white wine, and a quarter of an ounce of isinglass dissolved in a little water, and pour it into a mould.   This is a very nourishing jelly.

N

CAUDLE.

Make a fine smooth gruel of grits, with a few spices boiled in it, strain it carefully and warm as required, adding white wine and a little brandy, nutmeg, lemon peel, and sugar, according to taste, some persons put the yolk of an egg.

RICE CAUDLE.

Boil half a pint of milk, add a spoonful of ground rice mixed with a little milk till quite smooth, stir it into the boiling milk, let it simmer till it thickens, carefully straining it, and sweeten with white sugar.

BARLEY MILK.

Boil half a pound of pearl barley in one quart of new milk, taking care to parboil it first in water, which must be poured off, sweeten with white sugar. This is better made with pearl barley than the prepared barley.

RESTORATIVE MILK.

Boil a quarter of an ounce of isinglass in a pint of new milk till reduced to half, and sweeten with sugar candy.

MILK PORRIDGE.

Make a fine gruel with new milk without adding any water, strain it when sufficiently thick, and sweeten with white sugar. This is extremely nutritive and fattening.

WINE WHEY.

Set on the fire in a saucepan a pint of milk, when it boils, pour in as much white wine as will turn it into curds, boil it up, let the curds settle, strain off, and add a little boiling water, and sweeten to taste.

TAMARIND WHEY.

Boil three ounces of tamarinds in two pints of milk, strain off the curds, and let it cool. This is a very refreshing drink.

PLAIN WHEY.

Put into boiling milk as much lemon juice or vinegar as will turn it, and make the milk clear, strain, add hot water, and sweeten.

ORGEAT.

Beat three ounces of almonds with a table-spoonful of orange-flour water, and one bitter almond; then pour one pint of new milk, and one pint of water to the paste, and sweeten with sifted white sugar ; half an ounce of gum-arabic is a good addition for those who have a tender chest.

IRISH MOSS.

Boil half an ounce of carrageen or Irish moss, in a pint and a half of water or milk till it is reduced to a pint ; it is a most excellent drink for delicate persons or weakly children.

A FINE SOFT DRINK FOR A COUGH.

Add to a quarter of a pint of new milk warmed,

a beaten new laid egg, with a spoonful of capillaire, and the same of rose water.

***

A REFRESHING DRINK.

Cut four large apples in slices, and pour over a quart of boiling water, let them stand till cold, strain the liquor, and sweeten with white sugar ; a little lemon peel put with the apples improves the flavour.

***

A VERY FINE EMMOLIENT DRINK.

Wash and rinse extremely well one ounce of pearl barley, then put to it one ounce of sweet almonds beaten fine, and a piece of lemon peel, boil together till the liquor is of the thickness of cream and perfectly smooth, then put in a little syrup of lemon and capillaire.

***

A COOLING DRINK IN FEVER.

Put a little tea-sage, and a couple of sprigs of balm into a jug, with a lemon thinly sliced, and the peel cut into strips, pour over a quart of boiling water, sweeten and let it cool.

APPENDIX.

FRENCH METHOD OF MAKING COFFEE.

TAKE in the proportion of one ounce of the berries to half a pint of water, and grind them at the instant of using them. Put the powder into a coffee biggin, press it down closely, and pour over a little water sufficient to moisten it, and then add the remainder by degrees; the water must be perfectly boiling all the time; let it run quite through before the top of the percolator is taken off, it must be served with an equal quantity of boiling milk. Coffee made in this manner is much clearer and better flavored than when boiled, and it is a much more economical method than boiling it.

A FRENCH RECEIPT FOR MAKING CHOCOLATE.

Take one ounce of chocolate, cut it in small pieces, and boil it about six or seven minutes with a small teacup full of water; stir it till smooth, then add nearly a pint of good milk, give it another boil, stirring or milling it well, and serve directly. If required very thick, a larger proportion of chocolate must be used.

EGG WINE.

Beat a fresh egg, and add it to a tumbler of white wine and water, sweetened and spiced; set it on the fire, stir it gently one way until it thickens; this, with toast, forms a light nutritive supper.

MULLED WINE.

Boil a little spice, cinnamon, ginger, and cloves, in water, till the flavor is gained, then add wine, as much as may be approved, sugar and nutmeg; a strip or two of orange rind cut thin will be found a great improvement.

TO MAKE PUNCH.

To make one quart, provide two fine fresh lemons, and rub off the outer peel upon a few lumps of sugar; put the sugar into a bowl with four ounces of powdered sugar, upon which press the juice of the lemons, and pour over one pint and a half of very hot water that *has not boiled,* then add a quarter of a pint of rum, and the same quantity of brandy; stir well together and strain it, and let it stand a few minutes before it is drank.

Whiskey punch is made after the same method; the juice and thin peel of a Seville orange add variety of flavor to punch, particularly of whiskey punch.

MILK PUNCH.

Put into a quart of new milk the thinly pared rind of a lemon, and four ounces of lump sugar; let it boil slowly, remove the peel, and stir in the yolks of two eggs, previously mixed with a little cold milk; add by degrees a tea-cup full of rum, the same of brandy; mill the punch to a fine froth, and serve immediately in quite warm glasses. The punch must not be allowed to boil after the eggs have been added.

A FRENCH PLUM PIE.

Stew one pound of fine dried French plums until tender, in water, rather more than enough to cover, with one glass of port wine, and four ounces of white sugar, which must however not be added until the plums are quite tender, then pour them with the liquor into a pie-dish, and cover with a rich puff paste, and bake.

ROASTED CHESNUTS FOR DESSERTS.

Chestnuts are so frequently sent to table un-eatable, that we will give the French receipt for them. They should be first boiled for five minutes, and then finish them in a pan over the fire; they will after the boiling require exactly fifteen minutes roasting; the skin must be slightly cut before they are cooked.

TO ROAST PARTRIDGES AND PHEASANTS.

They may be either *piqué* or not; partridges require roasting rather more than half an hour, pheasants three-quarters, if small, otherwise an hour; they are served with bread sauce.

Partridges may be stewed as pigeons.

TO ROAST VENISON.

Wipe the venison dry, sprinkle with salt, and cover with writing paper rubbed with clarified fat; cover this with a thick paste made of flour and water, round which, tie with packthread white kitchen paper, so as to prevent the paste coming off; set the venison before a strong fire, and baste it directly and continue until it is nearly done, then remove the paper, paste, &c.; draw the venison nearer the fire, dredge it with flour, and continue basting; it should only take a light brown, and should be rather under than over-done; a large haunch requires from three to four hours roasting, a small one not above three. Serve with the knuckle, garnished with a fringe of white paper, and with gravy and red currant jelly, either cold or melted, in port wine, and served hot.

A VENISON PASTY.

Having baked or boiled two hours in broth, with a little seasoning, any part selected, cut the meat in pieces, season with cayenne pepper, salt, pounded mace, and a little allspice, place it into a deep dish; lay over thin slices of mutton fat, and pour a little strong beef gravy flavored with port wine into the dish; cover with a thick puff paste, and bake.

SALMON PIE.

Cut two pounds of fine fresh salmon in slices about three quarters of an inch thick, and set them aside on a dish, clean and scrape five or six anchovies and halve them, then chop a small pottle of mushrooms, a handful of fresh parsley, a couple of shalots, and a little green thyme. Put these together into a saucepan, with three ounces of butter, a little pepper, salt, nutmeg, and tarragon; add the juice of a lemon, and half a pint of good brown gravy, and let the whole simmer, gently stirring it all the time; also slice six eggs boiled hard, then line a pie-dish with good short paste, and fill it with alternate layers of the slices of salmon, hard eggs, and fillets of anchovies, spreading between each layer the herb sauce, then cover the dish with the paste, and bake in a moderately heated oven.

CHICKEN PUDDING.

Line a basin with a good beef-suet paste, and fill it with chicken, prepared in the following way: cut up a small chicken, lightly fry the pieces, then place them in a stew-pan, with thin slices of *chorissa*, or, if at hand, slices of smoked veal, add enough good beef gravy to cover them; season with mushroom essence or powder, pepper, salt, and a very small quantity of nutmeg, and mace; simmer gently for a quarter of an hour, and fill the pudding; pour over part of the gravy and keep the rest to be poured over the pudding when served in the dish. The pudding, when filled, must be covered closely with the paste, the ends of which should be wetted with a paste brush to make it adhere closely.

A FINE BEEFSTEAK PIE.

Cut two pounds of beef steaks into large collops, fry them quickly over a brisk fire, then place them in a dish in two or three layers, strewing between each, salt, pepper, and mushroom powder; pour over a pint of strong broth, and a couple of table-spoonsful of Harvey-sauce; cover with a good beef suet paste, and bake for a couple of hours.

The most delicate manner of preparing suet for pastry is to clarify it, and use it as butter; this will be found a very superior method for meat pastry.

———

AN EASY RECEIPT FOR A CHARLOTTE RUSSE.

Trim straitly about six ounces of savoy biscuits, so that they may fit closely to each other; line the bottom and sides of a plain mould with them, then fill it with a fine cream made in the following manner: put into a stewpan three ounces of ratafias, six of sugar, the grated rind of half an orange, the same quantity of the rind of a lemon, a small piece of cinnamon, a wineglass full of good maraschino, or fine noyeau, one pint of cream, and the well beaten yolks of six eggs; stir this mixture for a few minutes over a stove fire, and then strain it, and add half a pint more cream, whipped, and one ounce of dissolved isinglass. Mix the whole well together, and set it in a basin imbedded in rough ice; when it

has remained a short time in the ice fill the
mould with it, and then place the mould in
ice, or in a cool place, till ready to serve.

———

ANOTHER EXCELLENT RECEIPT FOR A FRUIT CHARLOTTE.

Line a jelly mould with fine picked strawberries, which must first be just dipped into
some liquid jelly, to make them adhere closely,
then fill the mould with some strawberry cream,
prepared as follows: take a pottle of scarlet
strawberries, mix them with half a pound of
white sugar, rub this through a sieve, and add
to it a pint of whipped cream, and one ounce
and a half of dissolved isinglass; pour it into
the mould, which must be immersed in ice until
ready to serve, and then carefully turned out
on the dish, and garnished according to fancy.

———

ICED PUDDING.

Parboil three quarters of a pound of Jordan
almonds, and one quarter of bitter almonds, remove the skins and beat them up to a paste,
with three quarters of a pound of white pounded

sugar, add to this six yolks of beaten eggs, and one quart of boiled cream, stir the whole for a few minutes over a stove fire, strain it, and pour it into a freezing pot, used for making ices; it should be worked with a scraper, as it becomes set by freezing; when frozen sufficiently firm, fill a mould with it, cover it with the lid, and let it remain immersed in rough ice until the time for serving.

ITALIAN SALAD.

Cut up the white parts of a cold fowl, and mix it with mustard and cress, and a lettuce chopped finely, and pour over a fine salad mixture, composed of equal quantities of vinegar and the finest salad oil, salt, mustard, and the yolks of hard boiled eggs, and the yolk of one raw egg, mixed smoothly together; a little tarragon vinegar is then added, and the mixture is poured over the salad; the whites of the eggs are mixed, and serve to garnish the dish, arranged in small heaps alternately with heaps of grated smoked beef; two or three hard boiled eggs are cut up with the chicken in small pieces and mixed with the salad; this is a delicate and refreshing *entrée;* the appearance of this salad may be varied by piling the fowl in the centre of the dish, then pour over the salad mixture, and make a wall of any dressed salad, laying the whites of the eggs (after the yolks have been removed for the mixture), cut in rings on the top like a chain.

THE TOILETTE.

___

CHAPTER I.

The Complexion.

___

THE various cosmetics sold by perfumers, assuming such miraculous powers of beautifying the complexion, all contain, in different proportions, preparations of mercury, alcohol, acids, and other deleterious substances, which are highly injurious to the skin; and their continual application will be found to tarnish it, and produce furrows and wrinkles far more unsightly than those of age, beside which they are frequently absorbed by the vessels of the skin, enter the system, and seriousy disturb the general health.

A fine fresh complexion is best ensured by the habitual use of soft water, a careful avoidance of all irritants, such as harsh winds, dust, smoke, a scorching sun, and fire heat; a strict attention to diet, regular ablutions, followed by friction, frequent bathing, and daily exercise, active enough to promote perspiration, which, by carrying off the vicious secretions, purifies the system, and perceptibly heightens the brilliancy of the skin.

These are the simple and rational means pursued by the females of the east to obtain a smooth and perfect skin, which is there made an object of great care and consideration. And it is a plan attended, invariably, with the most complete success.

Cosmetic baths, composed of milk, combined with various emollient substances are also in frequent use among the higher classes in the East; and we have been informed that they are gradually gaining favour in France and England. We shall give the receipt for one, as we received it from the confidential attendant of an English lady, who is in the habit of using it every week, and we can confidently recommend it to the notice of our readers.

The luxurious ladies of ancient Rome, who sacrificed so much time and attention to the adornment of their persons, always superintended the preparation of their cosmetics, which were of the most innocent and simple description—the first receipt we subjoin was one in general use with them, and will be found efficacious in removing roughness, or coarseness, arising from accidental causes, and imparting that polished smoothness so essential to beauty.

AN OLD ROMAN RECEIPT FOR IMPROVING THE SKIN.

Boil a desert spoonful of the best wheaten flour with half a pint of fresh asses milk; when boiling, stir in a table-spoonful of the best honey, and a tea-spoonful of rose water, then mix smoothly, place in small pots, and use a little of it after washing; it is better not to make much at a time, as when stale it is liable to irritate the skin.

A VALUABLE RECEIPT FOR THE SKIN.

Boil in half a pint of new milk a thick slice of stale bread, and a tea-spoonful of gum arabic;

when boiled, set it at a little distance from the fire to simmer almost to a jelly, then pass it through a folded muslin, and stir in a spoonful of oil of almonds, and the same quantity of honey, with a pinch of common salt; when cold it will be a stiff jelly. A little of this mixture warmed and spread upon the skin, about the thickness of a crown piece, and left on till it cools, will remove, like magic, all appearance of the dry scurf to which some of the finest skins are subject.

AN EMOLLIENT PASTE.

Blanch half a pound of sweet almonds, and two ounces of bitter almonds, and pound them in a mortar, then make them into a paste with rose water; this paste is a fine emollient.

A SUPERIOR OINTMENT FOR CHAPS, ROUGHNESS, ETC.

Mix with a gill of fresh cream a spoonful of beaten almonds; when perfectly smooth put it in toilette pots, and use as ointment for chaps, &c.; it will keep for a week if a little spirit of camphor is added to it.

WASH FOR PIMPLES.

Dissolve half a dram of salt of tartar in three ounces of spirit of wine, and apply with soft linen; this is an excellent wash for pimples, but, as these are in general the result of some derangement of the system, it will be wiser to discover and remedy the cause, than merely attending to the result.

LOTION FOR REMOVING FRECKLES.

Mix one dram of spirit of salts, half a pint of rain water, and half a tea-spoonful of spirit of lavender, and bottle for use. This lotion will often be efficacious in removing freckles.

COLD CREAM.

Warm gently together four ounces of oil of almonds, and one ounce of white wax, gradually adding four ounces of rose water; this is one of the best receipts for making cold cream.

A FINE SOAP.

Blanch and beat to a paste two ounces of bitter almonds, with a small piece of camphor, and one ounce and a half of tincture of Benjamin; add one pound of curd soap in shavings, and beat and melt well together, and pour into moulds to get cool; the above is a very fine soap.

———

LIP SALVE.

Mix together one ounce of white wax, the same of beef marrow, with a small piece of alkanet root tied up in muslin; perfume it according to fancy, strain, and pot while hot; the above is a fine salve for chapped lips.

———

CHESNUT PASTE FOR RENDERING THE HANDS WHITE AND SOFT.

Boil a dozen fine large chesnuts, peeled and skinned, in milk; when soft beat them till perfectly smooth with rose water; a tea-spoonful of this mixture thrown into the water before washing the hands renders them beautifully white and soft.

———

SUPERIOR MILK OF ROSES.

Boil fresh rose leaves in asses milk, and bottle
it off for immediate use; it will be found far
more efficacious than the milk of roses sold by
perfumers.

AN EXCELLENT RECEIPT FOR LIP SALVE.

Melt one ounce of spermacetti, soften sufficiently with oil of almonds, color it with two or
three grains of powdered cochineal, and pour
while warm into small toilet pots. We men-
tion the cochineal to colour the salve, it being
usual to make lip salve of a pale rose colour, but
we should consider it far more healing in its
effects without it.

A COSMETIC BATH.

Boil slowly one pound of starwort in two
quarts of water, with half a pound of linseed,
six ounces of the roots of the water lily, and one
pound of bean meal; when these have boiled
for two hours, strain the liquor, and add to it
two quarts of milk, one pint of rose water, and
a wine glass of spirits of camphor; stir this

mixture into a bath of about ninety-eight degrees.

SUPERIOR COLD CREAM.

Melt together one drachm of spermacetti, the same quantity of white wax, and two fluid ounces of oil of almond; while these are still warm, beat up with them as much rose water as they will absorb. This is a very healing kind of cold cream. The usual cold cream sold by perfumers is nothing more than lard, beat up with rose-water, which is heating and irritating to the skin.

PASTE FOR RENDERING THE SKIN SUPPLE AND SMOOTH (AN ENGLISH RECEIPT).

Mix half a pound of mutton or goose fat well boiled down and beaten up well with two eggs, previously whisked with a glass of rose-water; add a table-spoonful of honey, and as much oatmeal as will make it into a paste. Constant use of this paste will keep the skin delicately soft and smooth.

TO REMOVE TAN.

Cut a cucumber into pieces after having peeled it, and let the juice drain from it for twelve hours, pour it off, and add to it an equal quantity of orange flower-water, with a small piece of camphor dissolved in a wine-glass of soft water, bottle the mixture, and wash the parts that have been exposed to the sun two or three times in the twenty-four hours.

EAU DE COLOGNE.

Mix together one ounce of essence of ber-gamot, the same quantity of essence of lemon, lavender, and orange flower-water, two ounces of rosemary and honey-water, with one pint of spirits of wine; let the mixture stand a fort-night, after which put it into a glass retort, the body of which immerse in boiling water con-tained in a vessel placed over a lamp (a coffee lamp will answer the purpose), while the beak of the retort is introduced into a large decanter; keep the water boiling while the mixture dis-tils into the decanter, which should be covered with cold wet cloths, in this manner excellent Eau de Cologne may be obtained at a very small expense.

———

TRANSPARENT SOAP.

Put into a bottle, windsor soap in shavings, half fill it with spirits of wine, set it near the fire till the soap is dissolved, when, pour it into moulds to cool.

———

MILK OF ROSES.

Put into a bottle one pint of rose-water, one ounce of oil of almonds; shake well together, then add fifty drops of oil of tartar.

———

HUNGARY WATER.

Put into a bottle one pint of spirits of wine, one gill of water, and half an ounce of oil of rosemary; shake well together.

———

LAVENDER WATER.

Take three drachms of English oil of lavender, spirits of wine one pint; shake in a quart bottle, then add one ounce of orange flower-water, one ounce of rose-water, and four ounces of distilled water ; those who approve of the musky odour which lavender water sometimes has, may add three drachms of essence of ambergris or musk.

ESSENCE OF ROSES.

Put into a bottle the petals of the common rose, and pour upon them spirits of wine, cork the bottle closely, and let it stand for three months, it will then be little inferior to otto of roses.

ESSENCE OF LAVENDER

Is prepared according to the above recipe, the lavender being substituted for the roses.

SCENT BAGS.

Small bags filled with iris root diffuses a delicate perfume over drawers, &c. A good receipt for a scent-bag is as follows : two pounds of roses, half a pound of cyprus powder, and half a drachm of essence of roses ; the roses must be pounded, and with the powder put into silk bags, the essence may be dropped on the outside.

ESSENCE OF MUSK.

Mix one dram of musk with the same quantity of pounded loaf sugar; add six ounces of spirits of wine; shake together and pour off for use.

OIL OF ROSES.

A few drops of otto of roses dissolved in spirits of wine forms the *esprit de rose* of the perfumers—the same quantity dropped in sweet oil forms their *huile antique a la rose.*

CHAPTER II.

The Hair.

ALL stimulating lotions are injurious to the hair; it should be cut every two months; to clean it, there is nothing better than an egg beaten up to a froth, to be rubbed in the hair, and afterwards washed off with elder flower-water; but clear soft water answers every purpose of cleanliness, and is far better for the hair than is usually imagined.

One tea-spoonful of honey, one of spirits of wine, one of rosemary, mixed in half a pint of rose-water, or elder flower-water, and the same quantity of soft water, forms an excellent lotion for keeping the hair clean and glossy.

A fine pomatum is made by melting down equal quantities of mutton suet and marrow, uncooked, and adding a little sweet oil to make it of a proper consistency, to which any perfume may be added. If essence of rosemary is the perfume used, it will be found to promote the growth of the hair. Rum and oil of almonds will be of use for the same purpose. A warm cloth to rub the hair after brushing imparts a fine shiny smoothness.

As a bandoline to make the hair set close, the following will be found useful and cheap: take a cupful of linseed, pour over it sufficient boiling water to over, let it stand some hours, and then pour over three table spoonsful of rose-water; stir the seeds well about, and strain it off into a bottle and it will be ready for use; or take a tea-spoonful of gum arabic with a little Irish moss, boil them in half a pint of water till half is boiled away; strain and perfume.

To remove superfluous hairs, the following receipt will be found effectual, although requiring time and perseverance: mix one ounce of finely powdered pumice-stone with one ounce of powdered quick-lime, and rub the mixture on the part from which the hair is to be removed, twice in twenty-four hours; this will destroy

the hair, and is an innocent application. In
the East, a depilatory is in use, which we subjoin, but which requires great care in employing,
as the ingredients are likely to injure the skin
if applied too frequently, or suffered to remain
on too long: mix with one ounce of quick-lime,
one ounce of orpiment; put the powder in a
bottle with a glass stopper; when required for
use, mix it into a paste with barley-water;
apply this over the part, and let it remain some
minutes, then gently take it off with a silver
knife, and the hairs will be found perfectly
removed; the part should then be fomented to
prevent any of the powder being absorbed by
the skin, and a little sweet oil or cold cream
should be wiped over the surface with a feather.

CHAPTER III.

Teeth.

———

WATER is not always sufficient to clean the teeth, but great caution should be used as to the dentifrices employed.

Charcoal, reduced to an impalpable powder, and mixed with an equal quantity of magnesia, renders the teeth white, and stops putre-faction.

Also two ounces of prepared chalk, mixed with half the quantity of powdered myrrh, may be used with confidence.

Or, one ounce of finely powdered charcoal, one ounce of red kino, and a table spoonful of the leaves of sage, dried and powdered.

A most excellent dentifrice, which cleans and preserves the teeth, is made by mixing together two ounces of brown rappee snuff, one of powder of bark, and one ounce and a half of powder of myrrh. When the gums are inclined to shrink from the teeth, cold water should be used frequently to rinse the mouth; a little alum, dissolved in a pint of water, a tea-cup full of sherry wine, and a little tincture of myrrh or bark, will be found extremely beneficial in restoring the gums to a firm and healthy state. This receipt was given verbally by one of our first dentists.

Every precaution should be used to prevent the accumulation of tartar upon the teeth; this is best done by a regular attention to cleanliness, especially during and after illness. "Prevention is always better than cure," and the operation of scaling often leaves the teeth weak and liable to decay.

Acids of all sorts are injurious to the teeth, and very hot or cold liquids discolour them.

The best toothpick is a finely-pointed stick of cedar. Toothbrushes should not be too hard, and should be used, not only to the teeth, but to the gums, as friction is highly salutary to them. To polish the front teeth, it is better to use a piece of flannel than a brush.

P

Toothache is a very painful malady, and the sufferer often flies to the most powerful spirits to obtain relief; but they afford only temporary ease, and lay the foundation for increased pain. A poultice laid on the gum not too hot takes off inflammation, or laudanum and spirits of camphor applied to the cheek externally ; or mix with spirits of camphor an equal quantity of myrrh, dilute it with warm water, and hold it in the mouth; also a few drops of laudanum and oil of cloves applied to decayed teeth often affords instantaneous relief.

Powdered cloves and powdered alum, rubbed on the gum and put in the diseased tooth will sometimes lessen the pain.

Toothache often proceeds from some irritation in the digestive organs or the nervous system : in such cases pain can only be removed by proper medical treatment.

CHAPTER IV.

Hands.

—

Nothing contributes more to the elegance and refinement of a lady's appearance than delicate hands; and it is surprising how much it is in the power of all, by proper care and attention, to improve them. Gloves should be worn at every opportunity, and these should invariably be of kid; silk gloves and mittens, although pretty and tasteful, are far from fulfilling the same object. The hands should be regularly washed in tepid water, as cold water hardens, and renders them liable to chap, while hot water wrinkles them. All stains of ink, &c., should be immediately removed with lemon-juice and salt: every lady should have a bottle of this mixture on her toilette ready prepared for the purpose. The receipts which we have already given as emollients for the skin are suitable for softening the hands and rendering them smooth and delicate. The nails require daily attention: they should be cut every two or three days in an oval form. A piece of flannel is better than a nail-brush to clean them with, as it does not separate the nail from the finger.

When dried, a little pummice-stone, finely powdered, with powdered orris-root, in the proportion of a quarter of a tea-spoonful to a tea-spoonful of the former, mixed together, and rubbed on the nails gently, gives them a fine polish, and removes all inequalities.

A piece of sponge, dipped in oil of roses and emery, may be used for the same purpose.

When the nails are disposed to break, a little oil or cold cream should be applied at night.

Sand-balls are excellent for removing hardness of the hands. Palm soap, Castille soap, and those which are the least perfumed, should always be preferred. Night-gloves are considered to make the hands white and soft, but they are attended with inconvenience, besides being very unwholesome; and the hands may be rendered as white as the nature of the complexion will allow, by constantly wearing gloves in the day-time, and using any of the emollients we have recommended for softening and improving the skin.

CHAPTER V.

Dress.

———

In dress, simplicity should be preferred to magnificence : it is surely more gratifying to be admired for a refined taste, than for an elaborate and dazzling splendour ;—the former always produces pleasing impressions, while the latter generally only provokes criticism.

Too costly an attire forms a sort of fortification around a woman which wards off the admiration she might otherwise attract. The true art of dress is to make it harmonize so perfectly with the style of countenance and figure as to identify it, as it were, with the character of the wearer.

All ornaments and trimmings should be adopted sparingly ; trinkets and jewellery should seldom appear to be worn merely for display ; they should be so selected and arranged as to seem necessary, either for the proper adjustment of some part of the dress, or worn for the sake of pleasing associations.

Fashion should never be followed too closely, still less should a singularity of style be affected ; the prevailing mode should be modified and adapted to suit individual peculiarity. The different effect of colours and the various forms of dress should be duly considered by every lady, as a refined taste in dress indicates a correct judgment.

A short stout figure should avoid the loose flowing robes and ample drapery suitable for tall slight women; while these again should be cautious of adopting fashions which compress the figure, give formality, or display angles. The close-fitting corsage and tight sleeve, becoming to the short, plump female, should be modified with simple trimmings, to give fullness and width across the shoulders and bust, and a rounded contour to the arms. Flounces and tucks, which rise high in the skirt, are not suitable to short persons; they cut the figure and destroy symetry. To tall women, on the contrary, they add grace and dignity. Dresses made half high are extremely unbecoming; they should either be cut close up to the throat or low. It is, however, in bad taste to wear them very low on the shoulders and bosom : in youth, it gives evidence of the absence of that modesty which is one of its greatest attractions; and in maturer years it is the indication of a depraved coquetry, which checks the admiration it invites.

It is always requisite for a lady to exert her own taste in the choice of form, colour, and style, and not leave it to the fancy of her dressmaker, as although the person she employs may be eminently qualified for her profession, a lady who possesses any discernment can best judge of what is suitable to her style of countenance and figure.

In dress there should be but one prevailing colour, to which all others should be adapted, either by harmonising with it, or by contrast; in the latter case the relieving color should be in small quantity, or it would overpower the other in effect, as a general rule, sombre negative colours show off a woman to the greatest advantage, just as the beauties of a painting are enhanced by being set in a dull frame; still, there are some occasions with which the gayer tints accord better, and as propriety and fitness are matters of high consideration, the woman of taste must be guided in the selection of her apparel by the knowledge of the purport for which it is intended, always endeavouring to fix on that shade of colour which best becomes her complexion.

CHAPTER VI.

Effect of Diet on Complexion.

———

As the color of the skin depends upon the secretions of the *rete mucuosum,* or skin, which lies immediately beneath the *epedirmis,* or scarf skin, and as diet is capable of greatly influencing the nature of these secretions, a few words respecting it may not be here entirely misplaced.

All that is likely to produce acrid humours, and an inflamatory or impoverished state of the blood, engenders vicious secretions, which nature struggles to free herself from by the natural outlet of the skin, for this organ is fitted equally, to *excrete and secrete.* Fermented and spirituous liquors, strong tea and coffee should be avoided, for they stimulate and exhaust the vital organs, and interrupt the digestive functions, thereby producing irritation of the internal linings of the stomach, with which the skin sympathises. Water, on the other hand, is the most wholesome of all beverages, it dilutes and corrects what is taken into the stomach, and contributes to the formation of a perfect chyle.

Milk is very nutritious, it produces a full habit of body, and promotes plumpness, restores vigour and freshness, besides possessing the property of calming the passions, and equalising the temper.

Eggs are, in general, considered bilious, except in a raw state, when they are precisely the reverse; this is a fact, now so universally acknowledged, that they are always recommended in cases of jaundice and other disorders of the bile.

Spices, and highly seasoned meats import a dryness to the skin, and render the body thin and meagre.

Animal food taken daily requires constant exercise, or it is apt to render the appearance coarse and gross. It should be combined with farinaceous and vegetable food, in order to

correct the heating effects of a concentrated animal diet.

Excess as to quantity should be strictly
guarded against. When the stomach is over-
loaded it distributes a badly digested mass
throughout the system, which is sure to be followed by irritation and disease, and by under-
mining the constitution, is one of the most certain
methods of destroying beauty.

CHAPTER VII.

Influence of the Mind as regards Beauty.

———

ALL passions give their corresponding expression to the countenance; if of frequent occurrence they mark it with lines as indelible as those of age, and far more unbecoming. To keep these under proper *control* is, therefore, of high importance to beauty. Nature has ordained that passions shall be but passing acts of the mind, which, serving as natural stimulants, quicken the circulation of the blood, and increase the vital energies; consequently, when tempered and subdued by reason, they are rather conducive than otherwise, both to beauty and to health.

It is the *habitual frame of mind, the hourly range of thought* which render the countenance pleasing or repulsive; we should not forget that " the face is the index of the mind."

The exercise of the intellect and the development of noble sentiments is as essential for the perfection of the one, as of the other, fretful, envious, malicious, ill humoured feelings must never be indulged by those who value their personal appearance, for the existence of these chronic maladies of the mind, *cannot be concealed.*

" On peut tromper un autre, mais pas tous les autres."

In the same way candour, benevolence, pity, and good temper, exert the most happy influence over the whole person ;—shine forth in every look and every movement with a fascination which wins its way to all hearts.

Symmetry of form is a rare and exquisite gift, but there are other conditions quite as indispensable to beauty. Let a woman possess but a very moderate share of personal charms, if her countenance is expressive of intellect and kind feelings, her figure buoyant with health, and her attire distinguished by a tasteful simplicity, she cannot fail to be eminently attractive, while ill health—a silly or unamiable expression, and a vulgar taste—will mar the effect of form and features the most symetrical. A clever writer has said, " Beauty is but another name for that

expression of the countenance which is indica-
tive of sound health, intelligence, and good
feeling." If so, how much of beauty is attain-
able to all! Health, though often dependant
upon circumstances beyond our control, can,
in a great measure, be improved by a rational
observance of the laws which nature has pre-
scribed, to regulate the vital functions.

Over intellect we have still more power. It
is capable of being so trained as to approach
daily nearer and nearer to perfection. The
thoughts are completely under our own guidance
and must never be allowed to wander idly or
sinfully; they should be encouraged to dwell on
subjects which elevate the mind and shield it
from the petty trivialities which irritate and de-
grade it.

Nothing is more likely to engender bitter
thoughts than idleness and *ennui*. Occupations
should be selected with a view to improve and
amuse; they should be varied, to prevent the
lassitude resulting from monotony; serious medi-
tations and abstract studies should be relieved
by the lighter branches of literature; music
should be assiduously cultivated; nothing more
refines and exalts the mind; not the mere

performance of mechanical difficulties, either vocal or instrumental, for these, unless pursued with extreme caution, enlarge the hand and fatigue the chest, without imparting the advantages we allude to.

Drawing is highly calculated to enhance feminine beauty ; the thoughts it excites are soothing and serene, the gentle enthusiasm that is felt during this delightful occupation not only dissipates melancholy and morbid sensibility, but by developing the judgment and feeling, imparts a higher tone of character to the expression of the countenance.

Indolent persons are apt to decide that they have " no taste " for such or such pursuits, forgetting that tastes may be acquired by the mind as well as by the palate, and only need a judicious direction.

Frivolous employment, and vitiated sentiments would spoil the finest face ever created. Body and mind are, in fact, so intimately connected, that it is futile, attempting to embellish the one, while neglecting the other, especially as the highest order of all beauty is *the intellectual.* Let those females, therefore, who are the most

solicitous about their beauty, and the most eager
to produce a favourable impression, cultivate the
moral, religious, and intellectual attributes, and in
this advice consists the recipe for the finest cosmetic in the world, viz.—CONTENT.

Q

INDEX.
